# Tales from a Revolution

# New Narratives in American History

*Series Editors*
James West Davidson
Michael B. Stoff

# Tales from a Revolution

## Bacon's Rebellion and the Transformation of Early America

**James D. Rice**

OXFORD
UNIVERSITY PRESS

# OXFORD
## UNIVERSITY PRESS

Oxford University Press is a department of the University of Oxford.
It furthers the University's objective of excellence in research, scholarship,
and education by publishing worldwide.

Oxford   New York
Auckland   Cape Town   Dar es Salaam   Hong Kong   Karachi
Kuala Lumpur   Madrid   Melbourne   Mexico City   Nairobi
New Delhi   Shanghai   Taipei   Toronto

With offices in
Argentina   Austria   Brazil   Chile   Czech Republic   France   Greece
Guatemala   Hungary   Italy   Japan   Poland   Portugal   Singapore
South Korea   Switzerland   Thailand   Turkey   Ukraine   Vietnam

Oxford is a registered trade mark of Oxford University Press
in the UK and certain other countries.

Published in the United States of America by
Oxford University Press
198 Madison Avenue, New York, NY 10016

Library of Congress Cataloging-in-Publication Data
Rice, James D., 1963–
Tales from a revolution : Bacon's Rebellion and the transformation
of early America / James D. Rice.
p.   cm. — (New narratives in American history)
Includes bibliographical references.
ISBN 978-0-19-538695-0 (hardcover : alk. paper); 978-0-19-538694-3 (paperback : alk. paper)
1. Bacon's Rebellion, 1676. I. Title.
F229.R48   2012
975.5'02—dc23       2012023224

Printed in Canada on acid-free paper

*For Nancy Lee Clark Rice*

# Contents

# Contents

# ILLUSTRATIONS

# FOREWORD

Wʜᴀᴛ's ɪɴ ᴀ ɴᴀᴍᴇ? ᴏɴᴇ ᴏғ ᴛʜᴇ ᴍᴏsᴛ ꜰʀᴇᴏ̨ᴜᴇɴᴛʟʏ ʀᴇ-counted stories of early American history concerns the armed uprising that took place in 1676 in the English settlements of Chesapeake Bay. A Virginian, Nathaniel Bacon, demanded permission from the governor to lead an expedition against Indians in the backcountry and when that was denied, turned his ragtag army against Jamestown, the colony's seat of government. His name has been permanently attached to the events, now known as Bacon's Rebellion.

Certainly Bacon commands the center of the story, and James Rice provides a gripping narrative of the rebel's progress. But to label the proceedings "Bacon's Rebellion" is a bit like being content to illustrate the revolt with a portrait of the man, and have done. The gilt frame, centering our attention on Bacon, walls out entirely too much of the story, as Rice makes clear.

Consider: If the rebellion was truly Bacon's, why did it continue after his ignominious death, with rebel forces still raiding plantations, harassing English patrol ships, and refusing to surrender for several months? And if it is Bacon's Rebellion, why did neighboring Maryland, where the man was largely unknown, become a virtual powder keg, ready to explode in similar fashion?

Furthermore, how do the neighboring Indians fit into the tale? If Bacon frames the story, we ask why he attacked them and whether they were a threat, perhaps also contrasting the attitudes of Bacon and his followers with those of Virginia's governor, William Berkeley, and his supporters. But that approach leaves unasked the question of what the Indians wanted. Or more precisely, what was requested by the Susquehannocks, the Westos, the Pamunkeys, the Piscataways. . . . For in fact, each of those nations (and many more) possessed its own interests, which very much bear looking into.

Finally, a story of rebellion that ends with the death of Bacon fails to explore how the fears and demands of those who lined up behind him were resolved. That tale, spinning out over several decades, saw the English trade in Indian slaves being replaced by trade in Africans, witnessed the massive disruption of Indian peoples and cultures, and encompassed a "Glorious Revolution" in England that helped forge, for better or worse, a more stable British colonial identity.

In short, a full understanding of the rebellion requires replacing the framed portrait with a panoramic landscape. Rice takes us through that spacious territory with a narrative of three-dimensional immediacy, showing not just one tale from a revolution, but many: as Piscataways, English planters, slave traders, Susquehannocks, colonial officials, plunderers, and intriguers are all pulled into an escalating conflict whose outcome, month by month, remains uncertain. As events unfold, one of the rebels is warned that danger awaits if he continues. But it's too late to turn back. "I am in over Shoes," he replies. "I will be in over Boots."

Happily, we find ourselves in over boots too—and quite unable to turn back.

James West Davidson
Michael B. Stoff
Series Editors

# ACKNOWLEDGMENTS

For such a short book, I've accumulated quite a few debts. They start with Brian Wheel of the Oxford University Press and series editors James West Davidson and Michael B. Stoff, who solicited this book and supported it all the way. Jim Davidson, who took the lead in editing the manuscript, was simply terrific, and I have taken just about every last bit of his clear-eyed advice. Alice Nash's remarks on the original proposal profoundly shaped the direction this book would take, and Michael Oberg commented insightfully on both the proposal and the completed manuscript. Heather E. Barry, St. Joseph's College; Alan Bloom, Valparaiso University; John Fea, Messiah College; Max G. Geier, Western Oregon University; Stuart Leibiger, La Salle University; Maxine N. Lurie, Seton Hall University; Jack D. Marietta, University of Arizona; Jenny Hale Pulsipher, Brigham Young University; Martha K. Robinson, Clarion University of Pennsylvania; Robert M. Sandow, Lock Haven University; David A. Sicko, Mississippi State University, Meridian; Catherine L. Thompson, University of Connecticut; Natale Zappia, Whittier College, and several anonymous reviewers for the press provided further encouragement and direction. They will, I hope, see that I have taken their advice to heart.

One of the great pleasures of this project was that it took me so often into the field. Karen Miles of the Alice Ferguson Foundation met me early one winter morning to tour the site of the Susquehannock fort on Piscataway Creek. Mark Johnson gave an engaging and informative tour of Arthur Allen's home (now known as "Bacon's Castle"), while Troy Stavans allowed access to the grounds of Warner Hall. Archivists and librarians, too, made research trips productive and even fun: Dee DeRoche at the Virginia Department of Historic Resources was wonderful, as were the staffs at the Virginia Historical Society, Colonial Williamsburg's Rockefeller Library, the University of Virginia, the Library of Congress, Preservation Virginia, and SUNY Plattsburgh.

Conversations and correspondence with Warren Billings, Douglas Bradburn, John Coombs, Max Edelson, Matthew Gibson, Hilary Holladay, Henry Miller, Kevin Kelly, Julia King, Joseph Miller III, Philip Morgan, John Murrin, Helen Rountree, Brett Rushforth, Timothy Shannon, Owen Stanwood, Antoinette Sutto, Gabrielle Tayac, Lorena Walsh, and Stephen Saunders Webb made this a much better book than it would have been had I tried to go it alone. The members of the Rocky Mountain Seminar in Early American History, the Washington Area Seminar in Early American Studies, and the Upstate Early American Seminar at Binghamton University, though too numerous to name here, were no less helpful. Finally, this book could not have been written without research grants from the offices of the dean and president at SUNY Plattsburgh, Colonial Williamsburg's

Rockefeller Library, the Virginia Foundation for the Humanities, and the Virginia Historical Society.

Nor could it have been written without the love and support of my family. Emily Rice kept things in perspective, as children do: thanks, Emily, for getting me out of the office for those afternoon pizza breaks and cross-country meets! Patricia Heberer visited many of the places described here, listened to the stories contained in the book (sometimes more than once, I fear), and otherwise shared this journey into the seventeenth century. Finally, this book is dedicated to my mother Nancy Rice, who appreciates a story—and tells some pretty good ones herself.

# A Note on Language and Documentation

I HAVE RETAINED THE ORIGINAL SPELLING AND PUNCTUATION of the original sources, but have filled out abbreviations and converted some characters to their modern equivalents: "ye," for example, is rendered as "the," and "condiçon" as "condition." I also partially modernized dates. Before 1752 the British new year began on March 25 rather than January 1. I have converted dates falling between January 1 and March 25 so that (for example) February 1, 1676, became February 1, 1677. When Britain switched to the new calendar in 1752 it also skipped eleven days, but I have made no effort to correct for that: February 1 remains February 1.

Additionally, I have tried to keep footnotes to a minimum while also maintaining scholarly standards of documentation. Thus in the many instances where several paragraphs are based on a small number of sources I have inserted a footnote only at the end of the section. Rather than cite every single relevant secondary source, I sometimes refer readers to gateway publications—that is, fairly recent works that will point the way to earlier scholarship.

Finally, in the interests of accessibility I cite the published version of a document whenever possible, even if it contains errors of transcription. I have however consulted most of the originals, and in the few cases where the published version is hopelessly mangled I cite the manuscript instead.

# Tales from a Revolution

*Part One*

# "The Uproars of Virginia"

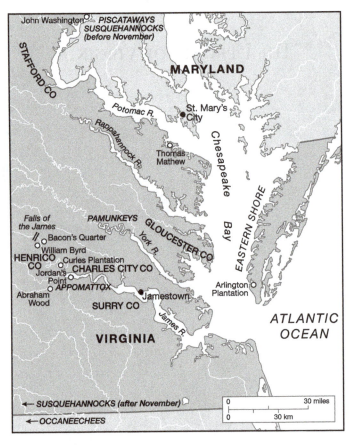

The Chesapeake Bay, 1675

## · One ·

# DOEGS! DOEGS!

THE FIRST FEW MONTHS OF 1675, IT SEEMED TO THOMAS Mathew and his neighbors, were filled with "Ominous Presages" of some impending disaster.

First came a sign from the heavens: from his home on the broad, tidal reaches of the lower Potomac River, Mathew watched each night for a week as a large comet appeared low in the southwestern sky, "Streaming like a horse Taile." Surely God had some reason for sending this sign, but what, Mathew wondered, could it be?

Then came the birds: massive clouds of passenger pigeons day after day in a seemingly endless column from one end of the horizon to the other. At night the slender, iridescent-headed birds nested on the branches to rest and feed on nuts and berries, periodically dipping down to the water to drink. Sometimes they settled so closely that tree limbs cracked and splintered under their weight, crashing down in an explosion of sound, leaves, and feathers. At night the hunters came out as well, casting nets over the drowsy pigeons before clubbing them to death or simply gunning them down, then feasting on pigeon meat the following day.

Old planters warned that the birds, like the comet, were a sign, a "Portentous Apprehension," of impending disaster. Planters in Mathew's neighborhood, as in most of Virginia and Maryland, lived on scattered farms linked by deep, slow-moving rivers and narrow paths or rutted roads. But they gathered regularly at small crossroads churches, or at quarterly meetings of the county court; they met on the roads, speaking to one another from high atop their horses to exchange news, or on the rivers, hoving to in their small sailing vessels or Indian-built dugout canoes to discuss crops and weather. The last such visitation of pigeons had been seen, they said, some thirty years earlier, "When th' Indians Committed the last Massacre."

The third "Ominous Presage" was disturbingly biblical. From millions of small, perfectly round "Spigot Holes in the Earth" rose "Swarms of Flyes"—locusts—"about an Inch long, and big as the top of a Man's little finger." Voraciously devouring the freshly sprouting leaves in the treetops, the grasshopper-like insects set up a deafening rattle. They descended to the earth again only to die, their dried-out husks littering the ground and heaping up along the foundations of planters' homes. In the Bible, visitations of locusts were disastrous events in which the large, bug-eyed insects swarmed over fields, devouring everything and leaving starvation in their wake. As biblically literate Virginians knew, they were sent by God as a chastisement.[1]

Even as he pondered the meaning of the comet, the birds, and the locusts, Mathew's own actions were setting in motion the "Attending Disasters" foretold by these visitations. Formerly a London merchant, Mathew had acquired a plantation near the mouth of the Potomac River at Cherry Point, nearly the widest point of any river flowing into the Bay, and had imported dozens of servants and slaves. He had also claimed lands upriver in Stafford County, on the frontier of English settlement. Some of it, no doubt, he intended to sell at a good price to later arrivals, or to leave to his children if he could find a wife. For the time being, however, he gave over at least some of his Stafford County acreage to free-ranging livestock, employing a herder to keep track of his hogs and perhaps cattle.[2]

Many of Mathew's neighbors were Indians: Chicacoans and Onawmanients from the Virginia side of the river, or Piscataways or Susquehannock Indians from Maryland, and others including the Doegs, displaced Indians from the many Indian towns that had lost their lands. Mathew and his neighbors traded often with the Indians, exchanging metal tools, cloth, and other goods for wild game, animal pelts and skins, dugout canoes, and labor.

The troubles began when Mathew "abused and cheated" some Doegs by "not paying them for such Indian truckle [trade goods] as he had formerly bought of them." Since Virginia's courts rarely provided relief for Indians, the Doegs retaliated by slipping across the river from Maryland, luring and trapping several hogs bearing Mathew's brand, hoisting them into their long dugout canoes, and paddling furiously for the opposite shore. An English boat set out in hot pursuit. It is easy enough to imagine the scene: a half-dozen men in each canoe, wearing breechclouts and perhaps soggy moccasins, their hair grown long on one side and plucked on the other, looking as if they were born with paddles in their hands, pulling with long, deep strokes, exhaling sharply with each thrust—confident at first, until they realized they were losing ground to the English sailboat, blessed with a favorable wind; then their world narrowing to near-total concentration on maintaining the pace despite the tightening of their triceps, shoulders, and backs as a burning fatigue in their muscles set in; and finally giving up, and turning to argue or fight with their pursuers.

As the Doegs turned, the English attacked. Again, it is not difficult to sketch in the details: the whistle of arrows from the canoes, the flash and percussive bark of snaphances and flintlock guns, the squealing of the pigs as they struggled against their bindings, the thud of arrows and bullets hitting home in wood or flesh; the cries of the wounded, the thrashing of those fallen overboard, and the spray of water and blood as the boats maneuvered for position and the bullets found their marks. Having recovered the swine, exacted revenge, and administered humiliating beatings to the surviving Doegs, the English returned to Virginia and allowed the Indians to limp home.[3]

The way Mathew chose to recall it, however, the story did not begin with stolen pigs or murdered Doegs. Instead, it began on a Sunday morning several weeks later, when a party of colonists on their way to church rode past the cabin of Matthew's herdsman, Robert Hen, and saw him "lying th'wart his Threshold, and an Indian without the Door, both Chopt in their Heads, Arms and other Parts, as if done with Indian Hatchetts." The Indian was dead. Hen, though bloodied by large gashes and slices, remained conscious. "Who did that," asked the churchgoers?

"Doegs," Hen croaked. "Doegs," again—and then he died.

Instantly the churchgoers sent messengers racing to notify Colonel George Mason and Captain George Brent of the Stafford

County militia. Mason gathered his horsemen and Brent his foot soldiers. They set out that evening with thirty men, following the trail of Hen's killers upriver along the south bank of the Potomac. The muffled steps of the horses' and men's shoes and the occasional clank of metal on metal broke the usual nighttime silence of the woods. After twenty miles, on the other side of the river in Maryland, the pursuers found the Doegs' landing. In the early dawn light they surrounded a nearby cabin. Brent called out in the local Algonquian language, demanding a "Machacomicha Weewhip," a council. The Doeg's leader emerged, trembling. Brandishing his pistol, Brent seized him by his scalp-lock and demanded "the Murderer of Robert Hen." The Doeg twisted away, but before he could go far Brent killed him with a single shot.

The Doegs in the cabin shot back and the English opened fire on the cabin. Under-armed, surrounded, and vulnerable, the Doegs "throng'd out at the Door and fled" through a withering fire. Soon ten dead or dying Doegs lay scattered across the forest floor.

Mason had already led the other half of the party to a second cabin nearby when the gunfire from the slaughter at the first cabin startled the inhabitants awake. Still sleepy and disoriented, the Indians rushed out into a hail of gunfire that killed fourteen men. One of the Indians ran to Mason, seized him by one arm, and blurted out "Susquehanougs Netoughs"—"Susquehannaugh friends"—and fled.

Susquehannocks? Mason panicked. Robert Hen had blamed the Doegs, not the Susquehannocks, for his murder. The Susquehannocks had been close allies of Virginia for nearly fifty years. They had been invited to live in Maryland in 1673 to serve as a buffer against the northern Iroquois enemies they shared with the Virginians and Marylanders. Mason was no friend to Indian people, but he realized that his men had just made a terrible mistake. Letting the Susquehannock man escape into the woods, Mason "ran amongst his Men, Crying out 'For the Lords sake Shoot no more, these are our friends the Susquehanoughs.'"[4]

The chastened Virginians retreated across the river, taking with them the captured son of the Doegs' leader. At Colonel Mason's home, the eight-year-old "lay Ten dayes in Bed, as one Dead, with Eyes and Mouth Shutt, no Breath Discern'd, but his body continuing Warm." Several days later Brent visited his "little Prisoner" at the Masons'. Studying the boy's condition, Brent saw sinister forces at work. "Perhaps He is *Pawewawd*"—bewitched— he suggested. If it was witchcraft, "Baptism was an Effectuall Remedy."

"No Minister cou'd be had in many Miles," replied Mason.

"Your Clerk Mr. Dobson may do that Office," Brent shot back.

And so gathered around the boy's bed Colonel Mason, Mr. Pimet (Thomas Mathew's overseer at his Stafford plantation), Mrs. Mason (as the Godmother), and the Roman Catholic Brent (as the Godfather), with Dobson officiating from the Protestant Church of England's Prayer Book. Dobson recited the Lord's Prayer and several others, then sprinkled water over the boy's head, saying "I baptize thee in the Name of the Father, and of the Son, and of the Holy Ghost. Amen." The group knelt by the bed and prayed: "We yield thee hearty thanks, most merciful Father, that it hath pleased thee to regenerate this Infant with thy Holy Spirit, to receive him for thine own Child by adoption, and to incorporate him into thy holy Church. And we humbly beseech thee to grant, that as he is now made partaker of the death of thy Son, so he may be also of his resurrection; and that finally, with the residue of thy Saints, he may inherit thine everlasting kingdom; through the same thy Son Jesus Christ our Lord. Amen."

The four men went back to chatting, smoking, and tipping back bowls of punch while Mrs. Mason cared for the child. To her surprise he soon opened his eyes and began to breathe normally, "wherat she ran for a Cordial" of medicine, "which he took from a Spoon, gaping for more."

Thomas Mathew called this miraculous exorcism "a Convincing Proofe against Infidelity." Like the supernatural portents that had preceded these events, the bewitching of the Doeg boy and the magical healing effects of his baptism kept alive the sense that there was something deeper at work, and more sinister, than a mere trading dispute.[5]

Long after Colonel Mason's mistaken attack on the Susquehannocks' cabin, the seasoned Susquehannock war leader Monges "still had tears in his Eyes" when he thought of the catastrophe it had set in motion. Though a young man when the attack occurred in 1675, Monges recognized the dilemma in which the Susquehannocks found themselves. Culturally Iroquoian, closely related to the Five Nations Iroquois of New York (the Mohawks, Oneidas, Onondagas, Cayugas, and Senecas), the Susquehannocks originally had made their homeland along the Susquehanna River. The rising power of the Five Nations in the sixteenth and seventeenth centuries, however, put the Susquehannocks on the defensive. They were steadily losing ground to the Five Nations, even with the aid of a close alliance with Virginia. But where to go? The Iroquois loomed to their north and west. Maryland, with whom the Susquehannocks had a somewhat shaky alliance, lay directly south. The Algonquian nations that predominated in Virginia and Maryland were radically different in their language and culture. They had long been enemies of the Susquehannocks, who had regularly raided the Algonquian nations for at least a century.

Maryland colonists, however, also had reason to fear the Five Nations and the increasing range of their raids. Thus in 1673, when the Susquehannocks finally admitted that they could not hold onto their homeland, their "great Man" Harignera persuaded Maryland's assembly to let them take up residence in the Piscataway Indians' territory along the Potomac, some twenty-five miles downriver from modern-day Washington, DC.

Harignera, young Monges, and their people struggled for the right response to Mason's attack on their cabin. The spirits of the murdered men had somehow to be "requickened," the ritual for anyone who had died prematurely or through foul means, or who left a particularly large hole in the community's life. Normally this would be done by warfare: at the behest of the leading women of the family of the deceased, men would go forth to take captives to be adopted in the place of the dead; this adoption might be ceremonial, after which the captives would be executed, or those so adopted might in fact live the rest of their natural lives in the Susquehannock community. But whom to attack in this case? If Monges and the other young men fell upon Virginians, they risked losing an important ally. If they captured Maryland colonists, they would be driven out and have to find yet another home. If they attacked the Piscataways or some other Algonquian

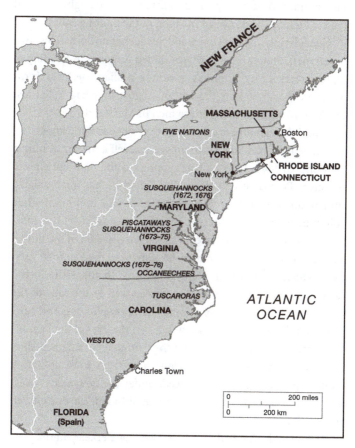

Eastern North America, 1673–1676

group they might also be expelled from their uneasy perch along the Potomac. And if they failed to act at all they might never fill the void left by the deaths of the men in the hunting cabin.

Considering that the Doegs and Susquehannocks had lost two dozen men, they chose a fairly restrained response. According to reports received by Virginia's governor William Berkeley (pronounced "Bark-lee"), by the end of August they had killed just two Virginians and several more men in Maryland.[6]

Could this handful of killings be overlooked? Berkeley, governor since 1641, had long since proved himself a master of Indian relations. In 1644–1646 he had suppressed the final uprising of the great Powhatan chiefdom. Since then he had manipulated Indian alliances to keep outright warfare to a minimum while still managing to dispossess many of Virginia's "neighbor Indians" of their lands and overseeing a rapid expansion in the Indian slave trade. In 1656, for example, he convinced the Pamunkey nation (which lived not far from Jamestown) to attack the Richahecrians, a northern nation that had moved to the falls of the James River. The battle was a fiasco, thanks to blunders and cowardice on the part of the English that cost the lives of the Pamunkey chief and many warriors, but the Pamunkeys remained allies and the Richahecrians nonetheless did refrain from bothering frontier planters afterward; indeed, under the new name "Westos," they became an important source of Indian slaves captured in Carolina.

The formula that had worked so well for Berkeley in the past, if applied to the Susquehannock conflict, would call for a measured response that did not commit too many resources to the conflict and made maximum use of diplomacy. And Berkeley was

Sir William Berkeley. Portrait by Sir Peter Lely, c. 1662 (Berkeley Will Trust, Berkeley Castle, Gloucestershire. Courtesy of the Virginia Historical Society)

accustomed to getting his way in such matters. Few colonial governors had enjoyed so much success and popularity. He had presided over an increase in Virginia's population from less than 8,000 to over 30,000, had held off invasion attempts by the Dutch, had worked extremely well with the colony's planters, and had kept Virginia in the king's good graces by remaining loyal to the Crown during England's Civil Wars (1642–1660) even after 1649, when Parliament had executed King Charles I and his sons had fled to France.[7]

In recent years, however, the aging Berkeley had found it harder to govern Virginia, and not only because he had grown hard of hearing and crabby from various physical ailments. Much of the trouble lay with Virginia's dominant crop, tobacco. Virginia's society, settlement patterns, and even Indian relations were built around the demands of growing tobacco. Tobacco encouraged dispersed settlement on scattered plantations. The growing population had spread into areas less convenient to Jamestown and beyond the governor's oversight. Younger, less established men had difficulty acquiring good land that was not exposed to Indian attacks on the frontier. In such places it was also harder to get one's tobacco to market. Moreover, overproduction drove down tobacco prices in many years, which great planters could ride out but put small to middling planters in a difficult position.

The key to economic independence was controlling labor, which was harder to come by than land. Growing tobacco was extremely hard work. Few people really wanted to work barefoot in Virginia's heat and humidity, hoeing, pruning back plants, and picking tobacco worms off the precious leaves, so planters relied on unfree laborers. Most planters had come to prefer slaves by the 1650s, but enslaved Africans were hard to come by and thus were owned primarily by elites: 90 percent of Virginia's officeholders owned slaves, but only 7 percent of nonelite planters owned any.

As had been the case since the founding of Jamestown in 1607, most newcomers to Virginia in the 1670s were still young Englishmen (and a very few women) with few other options in life. Most had agreed to serve as indentured servants for four to seven years. In exchange for their passage to America, indentured servants gave up their freedom to their masters. As long as they were servants they did the same work as slaves and lived under similar conditions, though unlike slaves they could look forward to their eventual freedom. If they lived, that is: the death rate, mostly from disease, was lower in 1675 than it had been in the early seventeenth century, but it was still startlingly high compared to rates in England and in colonies farther north. Even servants who survived to the end of their servitude were often chronically ill, for malaria, which weakened those it did not kill, was endemic in Virginia.

Even a servant who lived to the end of his term still might not be able to establish himself as a small farmer. Economic opportunities for ex-servants had been shrinking over the past generation. Many entered freedom already worn out from their years of servitude, reduced to working as tenant farmers or taking up small farms on remote, often dangerous frontiers. Fewer and fewer managed to acquire land and laborers of their own: in recent years the proportion of nonelite planters who owned any servants or slaves had abruptly dropped 20 percent from pre-1670 levels. Under these circumstances it was difficult to attract a wife from the small pool of unmarried women. Unable to establish themselves as married householders or to protect their families if they did manage to find a wife in a frontier area where the gender ratio was still heavily skewed, many freedmen were deeply frustrated at their inability to perform their roles as men. Their festering anger needed an outlet.

To make matters worse, Virginians faced a combination of low tobacco prices and rising taxes. The colony had already raised taxes to pay for an expensive lobbying campaign to rescind grants of millions of acres of land in northern Virginia that Charles II had made to private individuals. Additional taxes to pay the legislators' (the Burgesses) generous expense allowances during frequent assemblies were bitterly resented. Moreover, the colony was still paying for the Anglo-Dutch War of 1672–1674, when the Crown had forced Virginia to build a useless and expensive

fort at the mouth of the Chesapeake Bay. The fort had not prevented a Dutch fleet from entering the Chesapeake Bay in 1673
and sinking or capturing several ships. And not only were the
taxes high, the way taxes were collected—payable only in tobacco—was also burdensome. A growing chorus of complaints
blamed the commissioners of Virginia's county governments for
levying such heavy taxes, which unfairly burdened small planters
who grew little tobacco or had little to spare.[8]

Berkeley recognized that the colony's struggling planters (not
to mention servants and slaves) posed as much of a threat to the
colony as the Dutch did. As early as 1667 he had warned Charles
II to "consider us as a people press'd at our backes with the Indians, in our Bowells with our servants . . . and invaded from without by the Dutch." "How miserable that man that Governes a
People," he had complained, "wher six parts of seaven at least are
Poore Endebted Discontented and Armed." Many of the armed
men who turned out to fight the Dutch in 1673 were so poor and
disaffected that they might switch sides if the Dutch gained the
upper hand, "in hopes of bettering their Condition by Shareing
the Plunder of the Countrey" with the invaders.

Most planters were too young to remember Berkeley's earlier
triumphs as governor, and so they judged his performance based
on the colony's more recent struggles. There had already been
several aborted uprisings. Berkeley was not eager for an expensive Indian war that would require him to arm and to further tax
a restless populace.[9]

Also seeking to avoid such a war was Maryland's governor
Charles Calvert, who was even more vulnerable to a rebellion than
Berkeley. Maryland suffered from the same problems as Virginia,

and more. Maryland was a proprietary colony: in 1632 it had been given to George Calvert, First Baron Baltimore, by Charles I. The king's authority was mostly exercised, on a day-to-day basis, by Baltimore and his successors. The Calverts and many Maryland colonists were Catholics. England had been a Protestant nation since the 1530s, and had come to see itself as the leading defender of true Christianity against Catholicism. Catholicism, increasingly, was associated in the English mind with tyrannical, arbitrary rule; with absolute monarchies in which elected representatives and law courts had little power relative to the Crown; and with England's greatest rival, France. During the English Civil Wars the realm's small Catholic minority tended very strongly to support Charles I (and his two sons when they fled to France after the king's execution in 1649), while the most radical Protestants tended to support the rule of Parliament and then the "Protectorates" of the parliamentary soldier Oliver Cromwell and his son Richard until Charles I's son, Charles II, was restored to the throne in 1660.

To shield themselves from accusations of trying to reestablish Catholicism in English territory, the Calverts appointed Protestant governors and recruited Protestant settlers. The question was, would the newcomers be as tolerant of religious differences as their proprietor was? The answer was a resounding no. In 1660 the Protestant governor, Josias Fendall, led an unsuccessful coup against Maryland's proprietary government. Still the Calverts stuck with their strategy of conciliating Protestants: rather than hanging Fendall for treason they allowed him to stay in Maryland, keep his substantial landholdings, and remain an outspoken critic of the Calvert proprietorship. Other potential rebels took note of this leniency. Notable among them was John Coode, a former Protestant clergyman who had become a tobacco planter after he married a wealthy widow. Coode steadily took on more responsibilities, becoming a militia captain, justice of the peace, and eventually winning election to the colony's Assembly. Coode also became a close ally of Fendall and an increasingly virulent anti-Catholic opponent of the proprietary government.[10]

Clearly neither Berkeley nor Calvert could afford to raise taxes to pay for an Indian war. Yet neither could they afford to be perceived as putting colonists at risk by coddling Indians. As a steady stream of panicked dispatches from Stafford County brought word of armed Indians terrorizing the inhabitants, Berkeley realized that he had to order some kind of military response.

John Washington had only recently arrived on the Potomac River when the killings began. A well-connected native of Virginia's Eastern Shore, he came to the river to develop a 5,000-acre tract between Dogue Creek and Little Hunting Creek. Having filed the preliminary paperwork with the provincial government in 1674, he was anxious to erect a house and begin clearing fields by 1676, as required by the terms of his land grant. The property, later to be called Mount Vernon, included a high bluff from which one could see directly across the Potomac to the Susquehannocks' fortified town at the mouth of Piscataway Creek.

Washington and his new neighbors were confident that the Indians would soon disappear altogether, and they stood to benefit from an Indian war that would hasten this departure. Some, including Washington, had even obtained land grants that were conditional on the Indians deserting the land. Nevertheless,

Berkeley knew that he had no choice but to rely on local leaders to defend against further Susquehannock and Doeg raids. Virginia's form of government gave a great deal of power to the individual counties, extending even to some limited control over war and diplomacy; besides, the Potomac River was several days' hard travel from the capital at Jamestown.

Rather than entrust the task of defusing the situation to the notoriously anti-Indian militia officers Mason and Brent, Berkeley turned to the newcomer Washington and to Isaac Allerton, Jr., a prominent planter who had a history of getting along well with his Indian neighbors. Berkeley gave Allerton and Washington command of the county militias from northern Virginia, instructing them to investigate "the true Causes" of the troubles and to punish the killers.

Washington and Allerton, however, had no intention of investigating the causes of the conflict. The day after receiving their commission from Berkeley, they wrote Calvert to request that Maryland provide 250 horsemen for an "expeditious march against the Barbarous Enemy and to assist the Virginia Forces now prepareing to pursue their Enemyes the Susquehanough Indians." Governor Calvert read the Virginians' letter to his Council (which in both Maryland and Virginia served not only as the governor's cabinet, but also as the upper house of the legislature and as the colony's highest court). The Council immediately agreed to the proposal.[11]

The Virginia and Maryland militias converged on the Susquehannocks' fort twelve days later on September 26. The Marylanders arrived first, crossing a steep ravine near the fort, braking down a short slope, and, as the morning sun slanted in from their left, advancing the last quarter mile over a low rise to the south of the Susquehannock stronghold. To their left lay the mile-wide Potomac; directly ahead the fort; and beyond it the mouth of Piscataway Creek. Swampy ground flanked the fort on either side. Two miles up the creek was the Piscataways' main town.

The fort sat on a low bluff some eight feet above the creek, looking down slope on three sides. Its palisaded walls were fashioned from tree trunks that had been stripped of their branches and set vertically a good three feet into the ground. The trees were spaced several inches apart to allow defenders to fire through the gaps, and lashed together at the top. The soil used to anchor the palisades had been dug from outside the walls, adding a ditch to the defenses and making the walls appear that much higher. At each corner of the diamond-shaped fort a protruding bastion allowed defenders to fire parallel along the walls at anyone who came too close. An inner stockade protected the people and houses within from colonial fire. The only sally port faced away from the colonists, over the more easily defended slope down to Piscataway Creek.

To the Maryland commander, Major Thomas Truman, it looked as if only a hundred warriors defended the fort, together with perhaps another 400 women, children, and elders. Rather than wait for the Virginians he sent two men, Hugh French and Jonathan Shankes, to ask Harignera "to Come and Speake." Harignera, it turned out, had recently died, so the Susquehannocks sent several other men in his stead.

The meeting did not go well. The Susquehannocks brought out "an old Paper and a Meddall" on a black and yellow ribbon, "a pleadge of peace" given them by Maryland's governor as a "Token

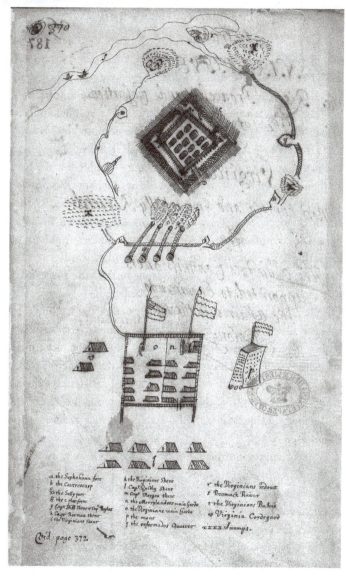

Siege of the Susquehannock Fort, sketched c. 1675 (Courtesy of the National Archives of the United Kingdom, C.O. 5/1371, 186)

of amity and friendship as [long as the] Sun and Moone Should last." Unimpressed, Truman ordered Shanks to tell the Susquehannocks "of the great Injuries that had been done to the Country" and to ask who had committed them. The Susquehannocks insisted that all of the killings had been committed by Five Nations Iroquois—a reasonably good story, as it deflected the blame toward the common enemy of everyone assembled at the fort. Truman called the bluff, asking that the Susquehannocks provide several men to pursue the northern Indians. When the Susquehannocks backpedaled, saying that the killers had a four-day head start, Truman retorted that since the Iroquois would not be expecting a pursuit the Susquehannocks might easily overtake them. At length the Susquehannocks agreed to the plan, but it was too late in the day to set out after the Iroquois.

When Washington and Allerton arrived at the head of Virginia's militia they found several dozen Susquehannocks still debating with Truman. The Virginians joined the argument, accusing the Susquehannocks of "the Murders done on theire Side." Impatient with the Susquehannocks' insistence that the Iroquois had committed the killings, some among the Virginians bluntly singled out three of the Susquehannock men as murderers.

This struck the Susquehannocks as a good time to return to their fort.

The following morning Susquehannock emissaries left the fort under a white flag of truce, hoping somehow to talk their way out of the siege. Again they displayed the peace medal and "old Paper." Washington, Allerton, and Truman, however, ordered the "great men" seized and bound and took them to the graves of the

Susquehannocks who had recently been killed by the English. Truman told the captives that they "deserved the like." Washington chimed in, asking "what[,] should we keep them any longer let us knock them on the head and we shall get the forte to day." The Susquehannocks "wer carried forth from the place where they were bound" and brutally clubbed to death.

The English, however, did not "get the forte" that day, nor the next day, nor the day after. Both sides settled into a long siege. English vessels patrolled the river and the creek, preventing escape or relief by that route, while on land the English hemmed in the Susquehannocks with a ring of breastworks connecting the spaces between the several small swamps and marshes surrounding the fort. Piscataway warriors and men from the nearby Mattawoman nation joined the siege, setting up camp at the rear of the colonists' position.

As the siege dragged into October and beyond, the colonists' initial confidence seeped away. The militia repeatedly failed to breach the walls of the Susquehannocks' fort. With each failure the momentum turned toward the Indians, who "often salleyed out, killed many and toke their spades and armes, and made themselves therewith stronger and stronger." Over the course of six weeks they picked off fifty of their besiegers and captured a number of horses.

Then, on a moonlit night in early November, the Susquehannocks stole away from the fort while the demoralized militiamen slept. As the Susquehannocks' noncombatants wended their way quietly between the swamps and the nearby encampments of the colonists, their warriors "knocked ten men o'th head, who lay carelessly asleep in there way," then burst upon the English encampment "hollowing and firing att them without opposition." The English failed to give chase until the following morning, and even then it seemed to at least one Virginian that they merely went through the motions. "For fear of ambuscades," he scoffed, they "would not overtake these desperate fugitives."

To some colonists it seemed as if the only possible explanation for the Susquehannocks' improbable victory was magic, some "wonderfull" power, "which doubtlesse was of some advantage extraordinary to them considering their Small Body." Perhaps, as the comet, birds, and locusts had hinted at the beginning of the year, powerful supernatural forces stood arrayed behind the Indians, and against the English.[12]

Far to the south of the Potomac lay the falls of the James River, a place that had long been an important crossroads for both Indians and colonists. Since 1646 Virginia had maintained a fort on the Appomattox River, just south of the falls of the James, commanded by a long-time Council member and militia officer, Abraham Wood. The Appomattox, which led southeastward across the rolling Piedmont toward the southern Appalachian Mountains, straddled a main path connecting Native American towns in the southeast with the Virginia colony and with Indian nations as far north as Canada.

Wood established a regular trade in which English packhorses carried arms, ammunition, and other manufactured goods into the Southern Piedmont each winter, returning in the spring loaded down with deerskins, beaver pelts, and Indian captives taken by their trading partners in raids against other Indian nations. The pelts and skins they tightly packed into giant barrels called hogsheads and shipped to England along with the previous summer's tobacco crop. The captives became slaves, working alongside English indentured servants and enslaved Africans to produce still more tobacco.

Wood enjoyed particularly close trading connections with the Occaneechees, a nation whose well-fortified town on an island at a shallow ford across the Roanoke River was an important way-station in the Indian trade. With the help of this strategic location, the Occaneechees partially succeeded in controlling Virginians' access to the southern trade. Only with difficulty were the English able to bypass them to trade more directly with the people beyond the river who actually hunted and processed the skins; indeed, other Native people in the region learned to speak the Occaneechees' language so that they could join in the trade.

The Occaneechees used their leverage as middlemen to obtain English guns and ammunition, which further strengthened their position. Wood thought that their power made them insolent, yet he continued to deal with the Occaneechees even after they killed one of his traders for having tried to trade directly with groups beyond the Roanoke River. In the sense that the Occaneechees and English were reliable trading partners whose mutually profitable relationship depended upon maintaining peaceable relations, the two nations remained friends.

Other Indian nations nevertheless competed with the Occaneechees, giving Virginia traders alternative sources of slaves, pelts, and skins while also establishing close relations with the new English colony of Carolina: the Tuscarora Nation, for example, who lived to the southeast of the Occaneechees near the Carolina coast, and the much-feared Richahecrians or "Westos," who since the 1660s had been raiding Indian and Spanish mission towns as far south as Florida and as far west as the Appalachian Mountains. The Westos had found the slave trade so lucrative that after their brief stay at the falls of the James in the 1650s they had decided to move closer to their victims, taking up new lands 400 miles to the south on the Savannah River but maintaining their connections to James River traders.

Wood faced increasing competition for this lucrative market in the 1660s and 1670s, both from Carolina traders and from his neighbors near the falls of the James—most notably, from Thomas Stegge and Stegge's young nephew William Byrd. Byrd arrived from London in the late 1660s and immediately took to the Indian trade. He roamed widely, exploring the Southern Piedmont and learning Indian languages alongside his uncle's trading employees. Byrd inherited Stegges's Indian trade and his plantation at the falls of the James in 1670.[13]

In 1675 Byrd had a new partner: Nathaniel Bacon. Bacon, born into a prominent family in Suffolk County, England in 1647, had spent the early 1660s wasting his father's tuition at Cambridge. After two years of Nathaniel's "extravagences" his father had had enough. He withdrew Nathaniel from the university and hired as his tutor a famous scientist, John Ray. Although Bacon was not the best of pupils (Ray described him as "a quick wit," but "impatient of labour"), the tutor nevertheless included Bacon in a three-year scientific tour of the European continent that eventually yielded a pioneering ornithological study. Bacon returned to Cambridge, earning his degree in 1668, then moved to London to study law.

Despite Bacon's status as the eldest son of a wealthy gentleman and his successful completion of his Cambridge degree, there were those who regarded Nathaniel with suspicion. Perhaps in part it was a prejudice against his family, which had included an uncle who rose high in the revolutionary government of Oliver Cromwell, Lord Protector of England during the 1650s. But perhaps it was something more, as well, something about Bacon's personal demeanor and ethics.

Bacon married Elizabeth Duke, the daughter of another Suffolk gentleman, in 1670. On the face of it, this was a good match between comparable families. Shortly before the marriage, however, Elizabeth's father rewrote his will, promising "unto my grand disobedient Daughter Elizabeth" a large inheritance upon her marriage to any man *other* than Bacon. She married Nathaniel anyway. Her father disinherited her and refused to speak to her again. It was a harsh act, but perhaps Edward Duke had accurately gauged Bacon's character. Soon after the wedding Nathaniel was accused of using his legal training to defraud a wealthy young neighbor of his inheritance. When the story came out Thomas Bacon suddenly recalled that his son, "having seen divers parts of the World before," loved to travel. He hastily shipped Nathaniel off to Virginia to escape prosecution. Elizabeth would follow after he had found a permanent residence.

Bacon arrived at Jamestown in the summer of 1674 with £1,800 in his pocket, enough to instantly place him among the colony's planter elite. There he established contact with two older cousins: Nathaniel Bacon, a wealthy planter and member of Berkeley's Council, and Frances Berkeley, the governor's wife. Bacon made a mixed first impression. His status, wealth, and connections won him a seat on the Council, but the dark, slender Bacon quickly earned a reputation for his "ominous pensive melancholly" and

"Pestilent and prevalent Logicall discourse tendinge to Atheisme." He adopted a reserved manner. When he did speak, it was said, he revealed "a most Imperious and dangerous hidden pride of heart, dispisinge the wisest of his Neighbours for their Ignorance." The young man, it seemed, was "very ambitious and Arrogant."

Perhaps it was for the best, then, that Bacon decided to purchase a plantation on the remote frontier near the falls of the James. Despite having lived and traveled in exceptionally cosmopolitan surroundings, Bacon explained to Governor Berkeley, he would be comfortable there; he had, after all, "always bin delighted in solitude" and, intriguingly, in "mistique imployments."

To Berkeley's annoyance, however, Bacon did not confine himself to solitary employments, "mistique" or otherwise. In September 1675, just as the crisis in Indian affairs was looming along the Potomac, Bacon attacked and imprisoned a group of friendly Appomattox Indians, accusing them of having stolen some corn. Berkeley rebuked Bacon for his "rash heady action." It was not Bacon's job to conduct Indian affairs. "The king hath committed cheyfely the care of the Country to mee," wrote Berkeley, not to Bacon. His rash behavior had only increased the prevailing "feare and Jelousie" among Virginians "that all the Indians were conspired against us." Such carelessness ran the risk of driving the Appomattox into the arms of the Susquehannocks and other enemy Indians.[14]

Berkeley, with years of experience at managing Virginia's elite planters and conducting Indian diplomacy, knew that headstrong young men such as Bacon had to be reined in quickly. He did not, however, foresee just how rash and heady Nathaniel Bacon could be, nor how talented he would prove at both inciting colonists and alienating Indians.

· *Two* ·

# THE SUSQUEHANNOCKS' DILEMMA

Breaking the siege of their fort on Piscataway Creek did not end the Susquehannocks' troubles, for the hundred or so warriors still had to shepherd to safety 400 women, children, aged, and infirm people and their possessions. Swinging around the Piscataway town at the head of Piscataway Creek, they walked upriver and crossed the Potomac safely above the colonists' settlements, then worked their way southward over the rolling Piedmont. Skirting the heads of the great rivers—the Rappahannock, then the tributaries of the York River, and the James—they avoided the colonial settlements clustered on the waterways' lower reaches. Encounters with other Indians were also to be avoided: many were trading partners and allies of the English, and most of them spoke tongues from the Algonquian and Souian language families, very different from the Iroquoian language spoken by the Susquehannocks.

Once clear of the English settlements the Susquehannocks found safety in the Piedmont, the wide expanse of rolling hills above the fall line—the place at which the wide lower reaches of the rivers gave way to shallows and rapids—but east of where the Blue Ridge, the steep front of the Appalachian Mountains, rose up. In this landscape of innumerable small streams, heavily forested with oak, poplar, and hickory trees, they could find enough food to survive the winter. By December the Susquehannocks had settled into several winter encampments: one above the falls of the James River and two others on the Roanoke River near the Occaneechees' town, a hundred miles to the southwest of the nearest Virginia settlement. Another small group went the opposite direction, taking refuge to the north of Maryland along the Delaware River. For the moment the Susquehannocks, though scattered, were safe.[1]

In the first days of January 1676 Susquehannock men returned to northern Virginia, passing undetected by staying to the west of the colonial frontier. Covering long distances on short rations, they soon reached the scattered homesteads near the falls of the Rappahannock. There they broke into smaller groups so they could strike simultaneously in a number of places. At each remote farm they found a similar scene: a small field, fallow at this season with patches of snow over the frozen ground, full of tree stumps; between the stumps, the remains of hundreds of small hillocks in which corn or tobacco had been planted the previous summer; and beyond the field a small, unpainted wood-frame house surrounded by packed dirt, a fenced-in garden plot, a horse pen, a small barn or two, and perhaps some other small outbuildings. A handful of people, mostly young English servants, went about their business.

At last, in a coordinated series of attacks, the Susquehannocks charged the colonists they had singled out, swinging an axe, drawing a bow, or kneeling to fire, cutting the English down as

Portrait of a Susquehannock. Sketch by William Hole, after Theodore de Bry. (From John Smith, *A Map of Virginia*, 1612. Courtesy of the Virginia Historical Society)

they worked or ran for shelter. Within minutes the attackers had melted back into the woods, leaving behind the bodies of colonists slumped over fence railings, against walls, or face-down on the hard winter ground. Having killed between thirty-six and sixty English, the Susquehannocks retreated to their winter quarters.

The Susquehannocks hoped that the matter might now be closed. A few weeks after the attacks on the Rappahannock they sent an interpreter with a message to Berkeley. What, the

Susquehannocks' chief asked, had caused the Virginians to "take up arms against him his professed friend" after nearly fifty years of alliance between them? The chief grieved that the Virginians had been "so eager in their groundless quarrell" and that Berkeley had permitted the murder of his peace messengers at the beginning of the siege of their fort in September. It seemed only fair to the chief, the interpreter reported, that he had "revenged himselfe by killing 10 for one of the Verginians, such being the disperportion between his grate men murthered, and those by his command slane." Now, if Berkeley would "allow him a valluable satisfaction for the damage he had sustained by the war, and no more concerne himselfe in the Marylanders quarill, he was content to renew and confirme the ancient league of amity" between Virginia and the Susquehannocks. If not, however, he was "resolved to fite it out to the last man."

Berkeley's Indian diplomacy had consistently favored the Susquehannocks, but he could not possibly agree to the Susquehannock peace proposal. It was contrary "both to honour and interess" and wildly out of step with sentiment among the Virginians. Besides, diplomacy had been rendered useless by events that occurred during the Susquehannocks' retreat from their raids.[2]

Nathaniel Bacon's thousand-acre plantation, Curles, sat on a peninsula jutting into the north side of the James River a half-dozen miles below the shallow falls that marked the western end of colonial settlement. Curles had been a working plantation since 1630, well before Bacon's arrival in Virginia in 1674, yet nearly two-thirds of the estate had not yet been cleared of woods. The fields were given over mostly to tobacco, corn, and, somewhat unusually for the time, a pen for Bacon's eighty sheep. Bacon also kept a half-dozen milk cows, a young heifer and bull, and a half-dozen calves, plus eleven horses. His two dozen swine mostly fended for themselves, but the horses and milk cows needed pastures and a barn; other outbuildings included a blacksmith's shop, a tobacco barn, and a springhouse for cooling dairy products.

A dozen servants and slaves worked the plantation. An Irish blacksmith named Peter labored at his forge and shoed horses, making the air ring with the clang of iron and scenting it with the smell of burning charcoal and molten iron. Another Peter, a forty-year-old, was the oldest of five adult Africans including "Blind Tom" and Kate, who had a young mixed-race child. The remaining five slaves, about a third of the people living at Curles Plantation, were Indians: Junn, a forty-year-old woman; sixteen-year-old Tom, eleven-year-old Nathaniel, and two four-year-old boys. Kate and her child had a room to themselves in the main house, and she seems to have worked there. The other Indian and black laborers could most easily be found, during the day, working the fields or tending to the livestock.

Bacon and his newly arrived wife Elizabeth lived in a brick home that they had added on to the "old hall" of wooden construction. The addition had walls of double thickness, a tile roof, and some flourishes such as a tile cellar floor and an arched or vaulted doorway. Buried in the foundation for good luck was an ancient Roman coin dating to the third century, an apt symbol of the Bacons' European origins, culture, and identity mingling with other material possessions that signaled their immersion in a Native, African, and colonial world. The Bacons lived much more comfortably than most of their English neighbors, even those of comparable wealth: they had plenty of beds, bedding, towels, napkins, chamber pots, kitchenware, and other comforts.

Bacon had also purchased a second property close to the falls of the James, just north of the river at Shockoe Creek, which formed a natural pathway around the falls and into the interior. The overseer at Bacon's Quarter cultivated an additional tobacco field, tended to "a great stock of cattle," and maintained an Indian trading post.

Bacon's Quarter proved easy pickings for the Susquehannocks. Warriors on their way home from the Rappahannock raids in January 1676 fell upon the outpost, killing Bacon's overseer and laying waste the plantation. Residents of other outlying quarters near the falls suffered the same fate, including three servants of William Byrd, Bacon's partner in the fur trade. Rumors quickly spread that the Susquehannocks had "devised a hundred ways to torter and torment those poor souls" by tearing out their nails, skinning them alive, or knocking out their teeth.

The tobacco crop that Bacon had counted on harvesting at his upriver quarter had to be abandoned, for "such plantation Nobody durst come nigh" as long as the Susquehannocks were abroad. All along the heads of the rivers planters began pulling back to more densely settled areas. "In these most frightfull times," Mathew later recalled, "small families withdrew into our houses of better Numbers, which we fortified with Pallisadoes and redoubts." Neighbors combined forces and took turns standing guard and working each others' fields. At Curles Plantation Bacon built a complex of trenches, underground tunnels, and fortified walls, and stockpiled weapons (including a basketful of hand grenades).[3]

In Jamestown an emergency meeting of Berkeley and his advisors dispatched councilor Sir Henry Chicheley to track down the Susquehannocks. Chicheley swiftly assembled 300 men. Catching the Susquehannocks would not be easy, even on horseback: as one of Berkeley's advisors pointed out, "they will burne a lone house or two to night and bee Forty myles off tomorrow." Still the English could no more allow the recent killings to go unrevenged than the Susquehannocks could have permitted the murders along the Potomac go unpunished; besides, even if Chicheley could not locate the Susquehannocks the presence of his army might discourage additional raids.

Thus Chicheley's men were stunned to learn, just as they were about to march, that Berkeley had canceled their expedition. The governor gave no reason for this abrupt reversal and postponed any discussion of the crisis until the March meeting of the Assembly. He offered no plan for protecting the frontiers in the meantime, "leaving the Poore Inhabitants under continual and deadly feares and terrors of their Lives." Many abandoned their homes altogether, including sixty of the seventy-one plantations in a single district along the Rappahannock River.[4]

Panic flourished in the void left by Berkeley's inaction. At Curles, Elizabeth Bacon heard every rumor that echoed up and down the river. The several dozen people killed in the Susquehannock raids swelled, through the power of gossip, to "neer three hundred Christian persons murder'd." A handful of attacks became "Frequent . . . Bloudsheds" and "Continuall Murders." The three killings committed at the falls of the James left the inhabitants convinced that they were about to die. "Wee are all afraid of goeing about our domesticall affairs," confessed several of Bacon's neighbors.

Governor Berkeley feared that something even more sinister than a falling-out with the Susquehannocks was afoot. Letters from the New England colonies brought the news that numerous Indian nations under the leadership of Metacom (also known as King Philip) had joined forces against Massachusetts, Rhode Island, and Connecticut. The Indians' highly coordinated attacks destroyed numerous English towns and forced New Englanders to "desert above a hundred miles of ground which they had divers Yeares seated and built Townes on." After nearly fifty years of settlement, the Massachusetts Bay colony suddenly extended barely twenty miles beyond the coastal port of Boston.

Berkeley became convinced that King Philip's War was spilling over into Virginia. The New England Indians, he heard, had "sent Emmissaries as farr as our parts to seduce our Indians to doe the like," and the Susquehannocks had offered "to hyre other nations of Indians" to join the attack. They were already gathering on the upper James River, "where they lye hovering over us." Virginia's "neighbor Indians," those living peaceably within the colony, were poised to join the conspiracy. There "is no doubt," he told a friend, that "they alsoe would be rid of us if they could but I thanke god they have not dared to show themselves our Enemies yet." Just to be certain, Berkeley seized the neighbor Indians' powder and ammunition.[5]

As March 7 approached members of the Assembly—the Burgesses who had been elected to the lower house of the legislature and the Councilors appointed by Governor Berkeley to the upper house—saddled up and picked their way along the narrow paths and roads leading toward Jamestown, their horses treading on fresh green grass as the scents and sounds of springtime filled the air. Others set out in small schooners down the colony's broad, slow-moving rivers, around the long peninsulas of the western shore, and up the James River to the deep-water landing close by the shoreline at Jamestown. Most legislators were familiar with the route, having traveled to sessions every spring since the last general election of Burgesses in 1662. Early arrivals settled into their lodgings in the cluster of brick townhouses, inns, and private homes on the western end of the small island where Jamestown had been established in 1607. Over meals and drinks they caught up with old friends, exchanged news from their counties, and speculated about how Berkeley would address the crisis.

As they strolled the streets of the small capital city the Burgesses rarely lost sight of the wide James River, the low bluffs of Surrey County beyond, and the narrow reed-filled marsh separating Jamestown from the mainland. Dozens of substantial buildings, many of brick, clustered at the upper end of the island, a rare sight to planters who lived in a world of scattered riverside farms and impermanent wooden structures. There were several former governors' houses, blocks of row houses, and an old brick church. A brick fort protected the statehouse, an imposing red-painted brick building joined to the east end of four substantial row houses. Built under Berkeley's direction in 1664 and 1665, the statehouse stood three stories high and had two wings separated by a central hallway.

The several dozen Burgesses gathered on the scheduled day in their spacious chamber on the upper floor of the statehouse and began by choosing a new speaker, Augustine Warner of Glouces-ter County, to preside. Berkeley and the Council entered the chamber and took their seats. A minister took the podium and reminded his listeners of their most sacred responsibilities, then prayed for their success in the coming session.[6]

At last Governor Berkeley arose to deliver his opening address, which all in attendance understood to set the agenda for the coming session. Given the perils that the colony faced, we may imagine the Burgesses falling silent, leaning forward to catch every word.

Berkeley's plan was simple. It opened with a declaration of war against "all such Indians who are notoriously knowne or shalbe discovered to have comitted the murthers, rapins and depreda-tions" of the preceding months. Since the Susquehannocks' "re-tirements are not easily discovered to us," Berkeley asked for a series of forts to be built at the heads of the rivers amongst the thickest frontier settlements. Horsemen would patrol between the forts while foot soldiers protected the nearby farms. The com-manders were authorized to defend the frontier settlements against the enemy, and also "if oppertunity present, pursue, follow and Fight them," but they were not allowed to attack an enemy town or fortification without orders from the governor. Indian allies were to be paid with trading goods for their regular service at these forts, plus bounties for killing or capturing an enemy Indian.

The Burgesses liked Berkeley's plan. It gave local commanders the flexibility to engage the enemy whenever the opportunity arose, but the requirement of getting Berkeley's approval before attacking an enemy settlement seemed a good way of avoiding a repeat of the troubles caused by Brent's, Mason's, Washington's, and Allerton's poor judgment the preceding summer. It focused attention on the Susquehannocks and discouraged other Indians from joining them. The Burgesses quickly approved the plan.[7]

Outside the statehouse, however, the forts were derided as yet another waste of tax money in difficult times. Berkeley, confronted with the "universall dislike of the People" for the forts, suddenly found himself under pressure to give frontier inhabitants the initiative against the Indians. More than one group of colonists declared themselves "redy to take armes in defence of our lives and estates" and asked Berkeley to grant them a commission to attack the Indians, for the "dread of the common approaching calamity made the giddy-headed multitude madd, and precipitated them upon that rash overture of Running out upon the Indians themselves."[8]

Berkeley refused all such requests, leading some to suspect that he was part of a conspiracy against the frontier planters. Colonists whispered that the forts were "meerly a designe of the Grandees to engrosse all their Tobacco into their owne hands" by converting taxes into government contracts. William Byrd's aunt Sarah Grendon spread the story that "every one must pay a thousand [pounds of tobacco] per head" for the forts—as much as a typical worker could produce in a year—and that if they could not pay in tobacco he would take their "cowes and featherbeds."

Nathaniel Bacon went a step further. The conspiracy, he told his neighbors, included the Indians themselves. He spread a rumor that Berkeley "monopolized a trade with the Indians and granted licences to others to trade" in exchange for a third of the skins (although in fact it was the county courts, not the governor, that issued licenses to Indian traders). Berkeley and his favorites, Bacon complained, provided the Indians with firearms, which had "proved soe fatall to these parts of the world, that I feare wee shall bee all lost for this comerce." To put it bluntly, Virginia had been "for a small and sordid gain betraied." He also believed that his own high birth carried with it a responsibility to take action in order to look after "the wellfare of the people here." In unguarded moments he was heard to say that "the next man or woman that he heard of that should be kild by Indians, he would goe out against them"—if necessary, without a commission from the governor.

In Charles City County, a few miles downriver from the falls of the James, one last rumor pushed planters to defy the governor. Hearing of "Several formidable Bodies of Indians cominge down on the heads of the James River," they began gathering as "Volunteers to goe out against the Indians." For several days in April the woods echoed with the pounding of drums calling the men of the county to gather at Jordan's Point, a spit of land on the south bank of the James just below the mouth of the Appomattox River.[9]

While the volunteers from Charles City County were assembling at Jordan's Point, Elizabeth and Nathaniel Bacon entertained guests at Curles Plantation. Captain James Crews, a close friend and neighbor, was there; Bacon's fur-trading partner, William Byrd; and Henry Isham, a Charles City County planter whose estate, Doggams, lay midway between Curles and Jordan's Point. As the liquor flowed, the four men lamented "the Sadness of the times . . . and the fear they all lived in." As they reached "a height of Drinking," Crews suggested that they all "goe over and see the Souldiers on the other side James River and to take a quantity of Rum with them to give the men to drinke."

Crews, Isham, and Byrd, it turned out, had already "laid the Plott with the Souldiers" at Jordan's Point. The volunteers gathered around Bacon and "all att once . . . shouted and cryed out a Bacon! a Bacon!" and begged him to lead them against the Indians. Crews, Isham, and Byrd egged him on, swearing that they would "drinke damnation to their Soules to be true to him" whether or not he secured a commission, so long as they could "take Revenge upon the Indians."

Bacon had in effect been rehearsing his acceptance speech for months in bitter conversations about the savagery of the Indians, the uselessness of the forts, the waste of tax money, and the governor's friendship toward the Indians and his small circle of favorites among the colonists. Now Bacon "enourag'd the Tumult" at Jordan's Point. A "large Paper" was produced, upon which he wrote his followers' names "Circular wise, that their Ring Leaders might not be found out."

Afterward it seemed as if Bacon must have had some magic at his disposal to have convinced his men to take such a dangerous step, some "Charme" by which he "conjur'd them into this Circle" and bound them "by an oath to stick fast together." If so, the charm held. Bacon crossed the James again to New Kent, "a County ripe for rebellion," to recruit more followers. Within days he had a force of 300 armed men at his disposal, "Prepared to goe out forth against the Indians."[10]

· *Three* ·

# THE GOVERNOR AND THE REBEL

Posseclay, chief of the Occaneechees, was uneasy about the presence of the newly established Susquehannock forts so close to his own people's fortified town at the ford on the Roanoke River. It was one thing for the Susquehannocks to trade occasionally in the Southern Piedmont, as they had in the past, but another matter altogether for them to live there. Their presence, and their search for allies and trading partners, was profoundly unsettling. As the Susquehannocks struggled to fit into their new environment, they inevitably made some missteps. Word soon spread that they had run afoul of "the other lesser nations of the Indians and so made them their Enimies."

The Susquehannocks were well aware of their precarious situation and their dire need of friends. In February 1676 Edmund Andros, governor of New York and New Jersey, heard that a Susquehannock emissary had approached one of his officers to discuss a treaty. New York was already locked into an alliance with the Five Nations Iroquois, the very people who had driven the Susquehannocks out of the north and into the arms of the

Marylanders just three years earlier, yet Andros eagerly embraced the possibility of taking in the Susquehannocks. He encouraged a small group to settle on the Delaware River, just within the southern limits of his colony. It was still only May 11, plenty of time to plant corn if they decided to stay. Perhaps, Andros hoped, he might convince the entire Susquehannock nation to return to the North.

The Susquehannocks also continued to search for Indian allies in the South. And where better to begin than with their closest and most powerful neighbors, the Occaneechees? But when Susquehannock emissaries asked the Occaneechees to join them in their war against the English, the request backfired. They had inadvertently forced the Occaneechees to choose between their English trading partners and the Susquehannock newcomers. Occaneechee messengers ran to tell the English where they might find the Susquehannocks.[1]

Berkeley could hardly believe that Bacon, so new to Virginia, had persisted in taking Indian affairs into his own hands, or that so many Virginians had joined Bacon's illegal army. The forts were being built as the Burgesses had directed, and men from the coastal counties were assembling to patrol the frontiers from those forts so that frontier planters might be free to stay home and guard their own neighborhoods. So why didn't Bacon call off his followers?

Letters flew fast and thick between the two men. Berkeley warned Bacon that he was in mutiny and ordered him to come to Jamestown. Bacon insisted that he desired "ever to be esteemed by your Honor as a loyall subject," but made excuses for staying away. The delay did not "proceed from disobedience," but rather from the need to dissuade others from disobedience. "Since my being with the volunteers," he assured Berkeley, "the Exclaiming concerning forts and Leavys has been suppressed and the discourse and earnestness of the people is against the Indians" rather than against the government.

Of course, the Indians also demanded Bacon's attention and delayed his coming to Jamestown. The frontiers needed guarding and the Indians living within the Virginia settlements also bore watching. "Are not the Indians all of a Colour," asked the Baconites? The "Common cry" was "awaye with these Forts, away with these distractions, wee will have warr with all Indians . . . wee will spare none." Many of the Pamunkeys and other neighbor Indians, fearing violence at the hands of their English neighbors, went into hiding.

Berkeley decided to "call Mr. Bacon to accompt." Declaring Bacon and his men rebels, the governor gathered several hundred men from near Jamestown to capture Bacon. Swinging inland around the wide mouths of the creeks along the north bank of the James and fording them where they turned narrower and less muddy, the party took several days to ride the fifty miles upriver to the falls of the James. Somewhere along the way Berkeley learned that he had missed Bacon, who had crossed the James and headed south, leaving behind a message that "I am just now goeing out to seeke a more agreeable destiny than you are pleased to designe mee."

The governor spent more than a week at the falls of the James, waiting and searching. Meanwhile he accused Bacon and his men of being bent on "the ruin and overthrow of the Government," suspended Bacon from the Council, and pledged to crush the rebels unless they submitted by the end of the month. He also offered to step down as governor. Perhaps, Berkeley conceded, it was time for a change. He dissolved the Assembly, called for Virginia's first new elections in fourteen years, and scheduled an extraordinary legislative session at the beginning of June. There, if the new Burgesses wished it, he would join them in petitioning Charles II "to appoint a new Governor of Virginia and thereby to ease and discharge mee from the great care and trouble thereof in my old age."[2]

Meanwhile Bacon was pushing southward with his volunteers through the Piedmont along paths well known to Indians but new to most of the English. They arrived at the Occaneechees' Island tired and low on provisions. Standing on the north bank of the Roanoke, Bacon looked across the water to three low islands, each several miles long and separated from one other by narrow, deep gaps where the currents ran especially swiftly. The Occaneechees' fort lay on the middle island, surrounded by peach orchards and fields of corn, beans, and squash. Two smaller forts stood close by, with higher, rockier, more heavily wooded ground rising above them on the far, southern side of the island.

Posseclay had already prepared for the encounter. A flotilla of Occaneechee canoes "wafted Mr. Bacon and his men onto the Island," led them to the fort, and fed them. Refreshed, Bacon turned the conversation to the Susquehannocks. He learned that they had two forts nearby: one, five miles distant, inhabited by at least thirty warriors plus women and children, and another fort, ten miles away, that contained "a very considerable number of men besides woeman and children." Bacon was eager to attack the smaller fort right away, but his hosts protested that "your men are weary, and want sleep, and [are] not fitt for service." The volunteers, they insisted, should "stay and Rest heer, and wee will Goe and take the Fort for you and bring you an account of it."

The Occaneechees attacked several days later, wiping out most of the 150 inhabitants of the Susquehannocks' town. Returning in triumph to the Virginians' encampment outside their own town, the Occaneechees displayed the scalp of the Susquehannocks' "King" and a small mountain of captured beaver pelts, which they quickly stowed away in their own fort. They also brought seven Susquehannock prisoners as a gift to Bacon, and asked "what he would have done with them."

"Kill them," replied Bacon.

The Occaneechees put the last seven Susquehannocks to death with "Exquisite tortures" by "running fyer brands up their bodys and the like" as their victims struggled against the overwhelming urge to give their tormenters the satisfaction of making them cry out or beg for mercy.

To the Occaneechees' surprise, Bacon wanted more. He expected Posseclay to provide food enough to see the Virginians home, and pestered him so insistently to turn over the plunder from the Susquehannocks' town that some onlookers began to think that the beaver skins were "the onely cause of the quarrell." Posseclay replied that his men had done all of the fighting and should have the plunder. Still Bacon persisted. As night drew near both sides prepared for a fight, moving into position and readying their weapons. The wrangling continued until well after midnight, until finally Posseclay agreed "for quietness sake" to divide the plunder. Posseclay slipped into the fort. For a moment there was an impasse as the Indians aimed at the English from the walls of the other two smaller forts. The English crowded up against the palisade walls near the portholes through which one could fire out.

At last one of the Indians snatched up his gun and killed one of Bacon's volunteers. The Indians and English jostling at the fort's entrance were now terribly exposed. As the English tried to retreat, five were overwhelmed by the crowd of Indians rushing to get into the fort, "hacking and hewing and cutting downe many of their Indian Enemies" before being trampled by the panicked townspeople. Outside the fort English soldiers gunned down women and men, children and elderly, Occaneechees and visitors from other Indian nations. The relief of those who found shelter in the forts lasted only as long as it took the Englishmen flattened against the walls to swing their guns up to the portholes and fire inside. "The groans of men, woemen, and children" could be heard even above the din of the gunfire, the "howling" of frightened and anguished villagers, and the singing of Occaneechees as they fortified themselves for battle or for death. Inside the two smaller forts many burned to death, asphyxiated as they crowded together to escape the flames, or were blown up when the flames reached the powder stores. Those who escaped were met by gunfire as they burst from the flaming buildings.

Posseclay had already lost "all his Treasure his wife children and ammunition" in the destruction of the smaller forts, and other men's losses were just as great. Around them lay the mangled bodies of their dead. The town, which until yesterday had been one of the most important centers of trade in the southeast, now lay in ruins. Around 4:00 o'clock in the afternoon, with less than a dozen women and children remaining in the town, Posseclay and twenty of his men gathered for one last offensive. At a signal they launched themselves into the field before the fort, running in a tight circle with pauses to load their guns and take aim at the Virginians firing from every direction. Posseclay and a dozen others were shot down, some of them tumbling down the river's bank into the shallows. The last half-dozen men escaped into the woods, abandoning the town to the English.

Bacon's volunteers did not pursue. They contented themselves with taking away what loot had not been burned, along with Posseclay's daughter and a handful of other prisoners. The Occaneechees had taken or scuttled the canoes, forcing Bacon's men to shuttle their horses over from the mainland so that they could ford the river and ferry their plunder across on horseback. An afternoon thunderstorm threatened, so the Virginians hastily abandoned the island before rising waters stranded them amid the wounded and the dead. Turning their backs on the unburied bodies of at least a hundred Indians and eleven Englishmen baking in the sun, the volunteers began the long ride back to Virginia.[3]

The volunteers reached the English settlements on May 18, making their first contact at Fort Henry on the Appomattox River. Abraham Wood, still commander of the fort and an active Indian trader despite having been bedridden for several years, watched as they rode in at dusk, their horses' hooves clattering over the stones as they crossed a small creek and spurred their way up the bank to the field where they made a late camp.

Early the next morning Wood was awakened by twenty muske-teers gathered before his home to demand the delivery of an Indian prisoner at the fort named Jack Nessom, calling Nessom "one of the proclaimed Enemies to the English." Still in his bed, Wood answered that Nessom was *his* prisoner. "The country would not bee soe satisfied," replied one of the armed men. Wood climbed from his bed and spoke through the window, commanding them in the King's name "not to breake my house open."

"Bee [not] soe hott for there was noe body cared for it," shot back Bacon's messenger.

"Neither doe I for you," retorted Wood.

Wood fenced with the men a little longer, daring them to attack. Finally Bacon himself appeared. Standing on a small hill so that he could see better into the window, Bacon berated Wood "with a great deale of Scurrillous language."

"I suppose the Major General hath power," said Bacon. "And I have some power to[o]."

"Fetch the prisoner," Bacon commanded his men, "for hee is a murderer."

Faced with a direct order, Bacon's men rushed into Wood's home. Finding the room where Nessom was held, they broke the irons with which Wood had imprisoned him, gathered up Nes-som's wife and children, and led them away to the Charles City County jail.[4]

Election day in Henrico County, May 25, began with a session of the county court. Men planning to vote later in the day filled the small frame courthouse, just above the bend of the river from Curles Plantation, as the session opened with a reading of the

May 10 proclamation declaring Bacon and his followers to be in rebellion. Before the sheriff could finish Bacon burst in with forty of his armed guard, "thretning him terribly If he proceeded" with the reading and snatching the proclamation from his hands.

Later that day Bacon and the other candidates for the new assembly stood and listened as each voter stepped forward and publicly announced his vote. Afterward Bacon said simply that "I was chosen by the country a Burgesse." Others told the story differently, saying that "Mr. Bacon goes to the Court howse with his armed men, where he procured himselfe to [be] choasen their Burgess." Whatever happened, Bacon and James Crews, the neighbor who had engineered Bacon's call to leadership at Jordan's Point in April, were chosen as Henrico County's two Burgesses.[5]

Winning the election was one matter; actually taking a seat in the Assembly after having been declared a rebel was another. Immediately after the election Crews raced downriver, covering forty miles in less than a day to plead Bacon's case before the governor. At Green Spring, the governor's showcase plantation several miles outside of Jamestown, Crews was shown to the dining room. Berkeley, Henry Chicheley, and the Reverend John Clough, rector of the Anglican church in Jamestown, awaited him.

Crews presented a tight-lipped letter from Bacon, brimming with frustration and mingling threats with declarations of loyalty. His actions had arisen from a higher loyalty to the King's peace, Bacon protested: he had "never in any thing aimed further than the Countrys quiet and prosperity and the destructions of all Indians [and] of all trade concerned with them." He claimed to remain loyal despite "all your threatenings against my life which are dayly brought to my eares"; in fact, Bacon wrote, he doubted that Berkeley had said such things, because for Berkeley to have done so would have been contrary to "prudence." He refused to believe what others said of "your Honors falshood Cowardice treachery [and] receaving of bribes," no matter how often he heard them—not even, Bacon slyly inserted, when they produced evidence of Berkeley's corruption in the governor's own handwriting. Nor did he believe that Frances Berkeley had really been spreading "scandalous and false reports" about him. She was too much the "Honorable Lady" for that.

Over the next several days relations between the two men broke down completely. On May 28, Bacon wrote despairingly that "my submissions are unacceptable my intentions misunderstood. . . . I am sorry that your Honors resentments are of such violence and groweth as to command my appearance with all contempt and disgrace and my disowning and belying soe Glorious a cause as the Countrys defense." Yet he still held out hope that he would have his way, asking again for a commission. Berkeley and the Council remained unmoved. They condemned Bacon's "rash, illegal, unwarrantable, and most rebellious" proceedings, while Berkeley pointedly observed that Bacon had lost more soldiers in one day at the Occaneecheees' fort than had been lost in the entire Anglo-Powhatan War of 1644–1646.[6]

On that note, with a week left before the opening of the new Assembly, the correspondence between the governor and the rebel ceased. Bacon prepared to take his seat as a Burgess, and Berkeley prepared to receive him.

Lost in this exchange was any mention of the prisoners taken by Bacon's men. What had become of Posseclay's daughter and the other Occaneechee captives? What had happened to Jack Nessom and his family, abducted from Abraham Wood's home? Bacon noted that Nessom had been sent to the county jail, but he said nothing of his family's fate. The county court records that might have recorded all of this were destroyed by fire two centuries later, during another civil war. Were Nessom and his son the two victims referred to in a letter describing how Bacon had "seized two Indians, a man and a Boy," tied them to trees, "and with much Horror and cruelty put [them] to Death, without examining their crime"? Even if so, we still do not know what happened to the rest of the family. Did they become slaves, like so many other Indian captives? As for the Occaneechees, neither Bacon's supporters nor the governor's could say much more than that they had brought back "some Few woemen and children prisoners which they dispose of at their pleasure."[7]

From the colonists' standpoint the Susquehannock War had been transformed into a struggle between the governor and the rebel, exposing divisions among Virginians that had previously lain mostly beneath the surface. For Indians, however, the looming confrontation between Bacon and Berkeley was not at the heart of the conflict. The question of their survival was. The Pamunkeys and other neighbor Indians who had fled their towns for fear of colonial vigilantes wanted to know when they could safely emerge from the swamp into which Bacon's men had pursued them, and whether they could do so in time to plant a summer crop. The Susquehannocks wondered where they could go after their defeat at the hands of the Occaneechees. The Occaneechees, for their part, wondered what had become of Posseclay's daughter and the other captives carried away by the English, and how they would survive if they gave up their island fortress astride the Great Trading Path between Virginia and the Southern Piedmont. Nathaniel Bacon had, in his own impulsive way, managed to turn the worlds of both Virginians and Indians upside down.

## · Four ·

# "I Am in Over Shoes, I Will Be in Over Boots"

❦

In May 1676 two sachems from the small group of Susquehannocks who had taken refuge on the Delaware River earlier that spring accepted an invitation from New York's Governor Andros to discuss a peace treaty. Crossing New Jersey overland and pausing at the ferry landing on the Hudson River the Susquehannock pair, Conacheonweedo and Sneedo, could see across the water to the cluster of 400 houses mixed with gardens and orchards enclosed by the city walls on the lower end of Manhattan Island. Tall, narrow buildings with Dutch-style gabled windows and red-and-black tiled roofs gradually revealed themselves as they drew nearer. A long wall along the Hudson ended near the island's tip, which was commanded by the weathered stone walls of Fort James. Clearly designed to repel seaborne invasions, the fort was built startlingly close to the waterside; forty-six guns lined its walls. The Susquehannocks entered through a gate on the land-locked north wall into an open parade ground ringed by a barracks, a church, and the newly refurbished governor's residence.

Reassuringly, Andros was willing to follow the protocols of Indian diplomacy rather than imposing a European style of negotiating. Conacheonweedo and Sneedo were greeted by the governor himself. After welcoming them, Andros offered protection if they came to live within his government and assured them that the Five Nations would set aside their generations of enmity. The Mohawks in particular, Andros told them, now considered the Susquehannocks their "brothers and children." Andros concluded by asking Conacheonweedo and Sneedo to think about what he should say to the Mohawks when he met with them a few days later. Rather than demanding an immediate answer, Andros did what was expected in Indian diplomacy: he gave each of his guests a new coat as a gift to signal the seriousness of his proposal and sent them to enjoy the meal he had arranged for them.

The following day Conacheonweedo and Sneedo reminded Andros that they were "but two" and "so can give no other answer than that they will goe to the rest of their people and tell them what the Governor said." But, they hastened to add, this did not signal any lack of interest. On the contrary: once they had returned to their own nation for instructions they would truly be able to speak for their people. When they returned they would bring presents so that their agreement would be properly sealed and made binding. After another meal provided by Andros, the Susquehannocks "departed well satisfyed."[1]

Even though the recent Indian troubles had started within a few miles of Maryland's capital at St. Mary's City, Governor Charles Calvert was largely in the dark as to the intentions of the Susquehannocks, of the neighboring Indians within Maryland, and of

Andros, Berkeley, and Bacon. Maryland's governor could not even be certain of how his colony's elected Assembly would approach the matter, since it had not met since January 1675. Much had changed since then: in addition to the Susquehannock War Calvert's father had died in England, making Charles, already the resident governor of Maryland, the new Lord Baltimore and Proprietor of the colony. The transition in his personal life and in Maryland's government took a full year to settle and required much of Calvert's attention. By the time he returned from London and called a new Assembly for mid-May, Bacon had already been declared a rebel and had attacked the Occaneechees' Island. Virginians were preparing for their new elections, and Andros was negotiating with the Susquehannocks. Meanwhile, Maryland's government had done nothing except to levy an extraordinarily high extra tax at the end of 1675 to pay for the siege of the Susquehannocks' fort launched by Maryland's Major Thomas Truman (Chapter 1). The tax had also gone to pay rewards for the colony's Mattawoman and Piscataway allies in the Susquehannock War. It was time, Calvert knew, to address the crisis.

The normally quiet town of St. Mary's City came to life in early May as it filled with legislators, petitioners, and those simply seeking more company than was usual on Maryland's scattered plantations, bunking with friends and relatives or crowding into the town's inns and taverns for several weeks of conviviality and political maneuvering.

One group of visitors, staying together at Jonathan Baker's inn, stood out from the rest. Conspicuous in their unusual clothing and speaking in a language that few Englishmen understood well, these guests were Piscataways, Mattawomans, and other neighbor Indians representing the colony's oldest and closest allies. They were in St. Mary's to see how that alliance was holding up. Would the assemblymen recognize their loyalty during the Susquehannock War, or show themselves unable to distinguish between Indian allies and Indian foes? In short, could these people be trusted?

The Assembly's first item of business was to impeach Major Thomas Truman for the "barbarous and inhumane Murder" of five Susquehannock emissaries the preceding September. Within hours of the session's opening ceremony the Council had organized a slate of witnesses and ordered Truman's arrest. A small committee of the lower house began reviewing documents and interviewing witnesses of their own. If the committee members felt the evidence warranted it, they would draw up formal articles of impeachment; then, if the lower house voted to impeach Truman, he would face a formal trial before the Governor's Council. If the Council found Truman guilty the case would go back to the lower house for a decision on his punishment.

This was all very encouraging to the Indian observers, but they could not help noticing that most delegates in the lower house seemed more anxious to disarm the neighbor Indians than they were to try Major Truman. The assembly had barely opened before the lower house had presented the Council with an "Act Prohibiting Armes and Ammunition to be sould given or Lent to the Indians"—to *all* Indians. Like the Virginia Baconites who were calling for the annihilation of all Indians within their colony, the Maryland assemblymen who passed the bill saw no difference between Indian allies and Indian foes. To the neighbor Indians' relief the upper house immediately rejected the bill, returning it with a warning that it would force "the friend Indians . . . to Joyne with the Indians that are our declared Enemies."

After a week-long investigation and debate, the majority of the lower house voted to impeach Truman. The Council swiftly tried and convicted him. The next step was for the lower house to pass a bill of attainder, a new statute that would decide Truman's sentence. But some there had not wanted him to stand trial in the first place, and many were not convinced he had acted so badly. The bill they presented merely levied a fine. Truman's hand had been forced, his supporters explained, by the "generall Impetuosity" of the thousand-man army of Virginians and Marylanders. "It appears," the assemblymen offered as their final word on the matter, that the crime "was not maliciously perpetrated or out of any designe to Prejudice the province, but meerely out of ignorance and to prevent a mutiny of the Whole Army."

Calvert and his councilors were livid. Murder was murder, they replied. And if Truman's mutinous army really did want the Susquehannnocks killed, then why, according to the very testimony that had been used to justify Truman's light sentence, did it "so plainely appeare that his first Comands for the killing of those Indians were not obeyed[,] and that he had some difficulty to get his men To obey him"? In only fining Truman, the assembly had committed "a great and Unheard of Wickednesse," and the councilors had no doubt that there would be "many English Murdered" by Indians as a result. The lower house, they warned, should "take notice that what is now undone lyes at theire doores and not with us."[2]

The Indian onlookers at the assembly were no friends of the murdered Susquehannocks, but they had good reason to worry about the attitude displayed by members of the lower house. The assemblymen seemed all too willing to suspend the usual rules of war and diplomacy when Indians were involved. They appeared indifferent to how their actions would be perceived by their Indian allies, and to the danger those allies faced if the Susquehannocks sought revenge. They seemed unable or unwilling to distinguish between Indian allies and Indian enemies. In short, the recently elected members bore a troubling resemblance to the Virginians who were rallying to Bacon's cause.

Virginian Thomas Mathew thought of himself as a planter and merchant, not as a leader. So when Colonel George Mason and Captain Giles Brent approached him to stand for election as a Burgess, Mathew protested that he had "never had Inclinations to tamper in the Precious Intrigues of Government." But Mason and Brent insisted, and in the end Mathew decided that it was not "Discreet to Disoblige the Rulers" of Stafford County.

In early June, then, he sailed down the Potomac and out into Chesapeake Bay in his small sloop, bound for the new Assembly at Jamestown. His fellow Burgess from Stafford County, Colonel Mason, had already set out by horseback. In St. Mary's City the lower house and council were battling over Major Truman's sentence for the murder of the Susquehannock emissaries, and in New York the Susquehannock sachems Conacheonweedo and Sneedo were meeting with Governor Andros. At Curles Plantation Bacon was gathering forty men to accompany him to Jamestown, while at Green Spring Berkeley had just posted a letter begging the king to replace him with "a more Vigorous Governor." But Mathew, living on Virginia's far northern frontier, had only the vaguest idea of these events. Before he arrived at James-town after a week's sailing he had heard little but "rumours like idle tales, of one Bacon risen up in rebellion, nobody knew for what, concerning the Indians."

Mathew approached Jamestown in the morning, keeping to the inside of the bend in the river to catch the eddies that would help him upriver and allow him to avoid the stronger current to his port. Catching the prevailing upriver wind he could sail close to the thinly inhabited lower end of Jamestown Island on his right until he reached the provincial capital at the western tip of the island. As he approached the town, Mathew later recalled, he was "welcomed with the strange Acclamations of 'All's over, Bacon is taken.'"[3]

All was over? Mathew hastened ashore to find out what he had missed.

Among other things, Mathew had missed the formal opening of the Assembly.

When Berkeley mounted the stairs and entered the Burgesses' third-floor chambers to address the new Assembly on June 5, he saw mostly men who had sat in the last, long Assembly and who also served, by the governor's appointment, as justices of the peace in their home counties. Berkeley also saw a few empty seats, since several of the thirty-nine Burgesses, including Mathew, Bacon, and James Chew, were missing. With Chew absent, only one of the men facing Berkeley on the first day of the session, Jamestown's Richard Lawrence, openly supported Bacon.

At this same moment Bacon and fifty bodyguards were setting sail from the Curles. They arrived the following afternoon and anchored close to shore near the statehouse complex. At Fort James,

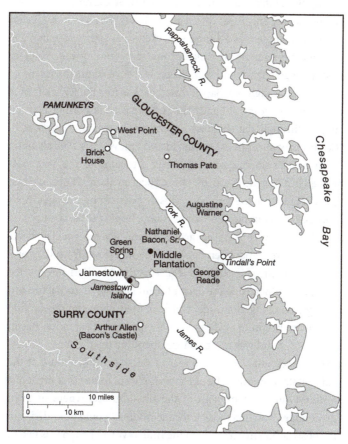

Jamestown and Environs, 1676

the solid brick structure built four years earlier to defend the town during the Dutch war, gunners trained their cannons on Bacon's sloop as a messenger was rowed ashore to ask the governor if Bacon could take his seat as a Burgess. Berkeley's answer was quick. He ordered the gunners to sink Bacon's ship, leading the rebels to hastily weigh anchor and seek shelter in a cove across the river.

Later, after nightfall, Bacon rowed back across the wide James to the capital. Landing at Sandy Bay, off the island's northern tip, he slipped through the shadows around the statehouse complex to Richard Lawrence's house to plan his next move. He stayed all night.

At dawn someone spotted Bacon returning to the longboats stashed just outside the town. Drums beat an alarm as Bacon's men rowed madly for the far shore, closely pursued by the governor's men. Bacon scrambled aboard his sloop, hoping to escape upriver, but the tide was running against him. Several smaller boats manned by rebel oarsmen began towing the sloop from the cove. Not in time: the ship *Adam & Eve*, captained by Berkeley loyalist Thomas Gardner, rode the current from Jamestown to Bacon's anchorage. Drawing alongside, Gardner fired upon the rebels' ship and forced Bacon to anchor. After a tense daylong standoff Bacon surrendered and was taken ashore, spending the night in a Jamestown jail cell attached to the rear of Berkeley's townhouse at the end of statehouse row. The old governor went to bed that night just upstairs, fully in command of the situation. Elsewhere in town "great hopes was, that those intestine troubles would be ended, and noe obstruction in carrying on the Indian Warr." Bacon was taken! The only question was, what would become of him?[4]

When Mathew arrived that question had yet to be answered. Bacon might be hanged for treason, but Berkeley also had

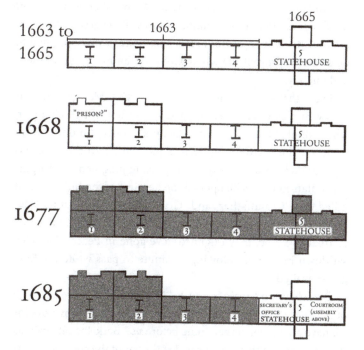

Plan of the Statehouse Complex. Units 1–4 were private homes; Governor William Berkeley's townhouse was on the far left, near the waterside and at the opposite end of the row from the statehouse. Attached to the rear of Berkeley's townhouse was the room in which Bacon was likely imprisoned at the beginning of the June Assembly. The darkened sections indicate portions of the building that were destroyed during Bacon's Rebellion. The plan for 1685 shows the partial rebuilding of the complex. (Courtesy of Preservation Virginia)

reason to worry. Two thousand men, he heard, were on their way to Jamestown to rescue the rebel. More sober estimates put the figure at 600, but that number was still far greater than the guard of forty men at Berkeley's command. Something had to be done to "prevent the whole Country falling . . . into ashes," and quickly.

Later that day the newly arrived novice Mathew and his fellow Burgesses trooped downstairs to the Council chamber, which doubled as the colony's General Court. No one was on trial, but the surroundings lent a judicial air to the proceedings. Berkeley was not shy about passing judgment on Virginia's Indian-killers as he opened the hearing. If the Indians "had killed my Grandfather and Grandmother, my father and Mother and all of my friends," he scolded, "yet if they had come to treat of Peace, they ought to have gone in Peace." Berkeley sat down in silence, allowing a minute to pass while the Burgesses waited.

Berkeley stood again to speak. "If there be joy in the presence of the angels over one sinner that repenteth, there is joy now, for we have a penitent sinner come before us." Berkeley sat again as Bacon came forward and kneeled at the bar of the court. Presenting a written confession and abject apology, Bacon swore allegiance to the king and his government. Berkeley allowed Bacon's concluding words, "begging Pardon of God the King and the Governour," to hang in the air for a few moments. Then, still sitting, the governor spoke:

> God forgive you, I forgive you
> God forgive you, I forgive you
> God forgive you, I forgive you.

The audience stood in silence on the broad plank floors of the chamber. Finally Berkeley broke the tension by pointing to the seat that Bacon had occupied when sitting in the Governor's Council, saying, "Mr. Bacon! if you will live Civilly but till next Quarter Court (doubling the Words) but till next Quarter Court, Ile promise to restore you againe to your Place There."

Mathew was so moved by the ceremony that he remembered it vividly, though surely imperfectly, nearly thirty years later. He was even more struck, however, by what happened next. Later that day, he recalled, "passing by the Court door, in my Way up to our Chamber, I saw Mr. Bacon on his quondam Seat with the Governour and Councill." It seemed, Mathew thought, "a Marvelous Indulgence" for a rebel who had just been pardoned for a capital offense to be restored to his Council seat so far in advance of the promised date.[5]

Some in Jamestown may have forgotten, amid the drama surrounding Bacon, that what was really at stake was the future of the Indian nations across a vast arc of territory from New York to Carolina. Not so Cockacoeske, the weroansqua—hereditary chief—of the Pamunkeys. Cockacoeske was well aware that if Bacon had his way her people would be scattered and destroyed, and that if Berkeley prevailed they could return to their lands and to their protected status as allies to the colony. The decision between these two alternatives, however, lay in the hands of the Assembly.

Berkeley wanted all other legislation set aside "untill the Indian Business was Dispatch't," pressing the Burgesses to form a joint "Committee for the Indian Affairs" with the upper house to hasten the drafting of a new bill. They agreed; thus, a few days later, Cockacoeske found herself standing with a small retinue outside the committee's chamber, waiting to be called as the first witness before a varied group of councilors and Burgesses that included Thomas Mathew.

Mathew was deeply impressed by Cockacoeske's performance. It began with her clothing: she could have worn English fabrics, as she often did, but instead she dressed as a werowance on a formal state occasion, wearing a crown of black and white beads, symbolizing spiritual and earthly power, and a long deerskin mantle with six-inch fringes. Mathew could not help but admire her graceful carriage as she entered the chamber with an English interpreter on her left and her son on her right, walked the length of the room, and seated herself at the lower end of the table.

Cockacoeske's "Majestick Air" and "grave Courtlike Gestures," however, were wasted on the committee's chairman, who abruptly asked her "what men she would Lend us for Guides in the Wilderness and to assist us against our Enemy Indians." She spoke "with an earnest passionate Countenance as if Tears were ready to Gush out and a fervent sort of expression," the torrent of words tumbling out so quickly that the interpreter could not keep up with her. But Mathew was able to make out Cockacoeske's repeated refrain of "*Tatapatamoi Chepiak*," or "Tatapamoi dead." Next to Mathew, councilor Edward Hill shook his head in sorrow. "All she said," explained Hill, "was too true to our Shame." Long ago, Cockacoeske's husband Totopotomy "had Led a Hundred of his Indians in help to th' English against our former Enemy Indians, and was there Slaine with most of his men." Hill understood perfectly well why "she now upbraided us": the English had never properly thanked or compensated her for that sacrifice, yet now they were demanding more.

"What Indians will you now Contribute," was the chairman's only response.

Cockacoeske responded with a "disdainfull aspect, and turning her head half a side, Sate mute." The chairman repeated his question. Finally, "that same Question being Press'd, a Third time," she replied "with a low slighting Voice in her own language" and with her head still turned away from the Englishmen:

"Six."

Cockacoeske sat silently and "a little while sullen," as the chairman continued badgering her, then spoke again:

"Twelve."

Then, as an admiring Mathew watched, Cockacoeske "rose up and gravely Walked away, as not pleased with her Treatment."

The freshly elected Burgesses were no friends to the Indians, but as they set out to draft the first bill of the session, "An act for carrying on a warre against the barbarous Indians," it became apparent that Berkeley's measured and discriminating response to the Susquehannock War had more support than Bacon's call for a war of extermination. Even as the bill declared war in response to the "violent incursions" of the "barbarous Indians," its authors also confessed that "wee are not altogether satisfied that all Indians are combined against us." The "rules of our sacred religion, as those of humantie," concluded the preamble, taught that "we ought not to involve the innocent with the guiltie." Having thus decided upon a general plan of action that

Bacon was bound to reject, the Burgesses spent the next few days hammering out the counties' contributions of men and supplies.[6]

Bacon also doubtless disagreed with the Burgesses' declaration that Berkeley "hath for many yeares most wisely, gratiously Lovingly and justly governed this whole Country." Begging Berkeley to remain governor, the Burgesses refused to endorse Berkeley's request to retire, "but on the Contrary in all humblenesse and due Submission earnestly petition his most Sacred Majesty that he will gratiously please still to continue Sir *William Berkeley* Knight as our honorable Governor."[7]

After his restoration to the Council it began to dawn on Bacon that his cause was not yet lost. Granted, he had no allies on the Council, and the Burgesses had repudiated his Indian policy. But he did have Berkeley's promise of a commission to go out against the Indians, and, as he soon learned, there were "an incredible Number" of people prepared to join in his cause.

When Berkeley did not immediately deliver a commission, Bacon concluded that it had all been a trick designed to pacify his followers. Besides, if Berkeley ever did sign a commission, Bacon suspected, it would be worded to prevent him from attacking the Pamunkeys and other Indian allies. What good was such a commission, he wondered? He could not fathom "this fatall undistinguishable distinction" between Indian allies and Indian enemies.

Several days after Bacon's submission Mathew was awakened early by cries of "Bacon is fled, Bacon is fled"! Curious, he went directly to the home of Richard Lawrence. Bacon, Lawrence told

Mathew, had left before daybreak after being tipped off by the older Nathaniel Bacon to flee. It had been Berkeley's plan all along, Lawrence believed, to wait until the men converging on Jamestown to rescue Bacon had gone home, then to retake Bacon, raise the militia to intimidate his defenders, and put him on trial for his life.

Despite the tumult surrounding Bacon's escape the Burgesses went about their business, swiftly drafting eighteen new bills and issuing a variety of directives. Some measures such as the "Act for the further prevention of mischief from unrulie horses," were not particularly controversial. Others transferred some of the power of the local elites who controlled county governments to ordinary planters and provided other means of relief from burdensome local taxes. Still others completely undercut Bacon's cause by interjecting diplomacy into Indian affairs, stripping Bacon of his offices, and reaffirming Berkeley's power to act against "certain ill disposed and disaffected people" who had "of late gathered and may again gather themselves together by beate of drumme." By the evening of June 22, a Thursday, all that remained of the legislative session was to read aloud in the lower house the final versions of the bills to be forwarded to the governor and Council for their approval.

At that moment, news arrived that Bacon was approaching Jamestown at the head of at least 400 men.[8]

The main body of Bacon's horsemen and foot soldiers arrived the next afternoon. Most assembled on the green near the statehouse, while others "Possest themselves of all the Avenues, Disarming all in Town" and intercepted men on their way to defend the governor and Burgesses. Drums began to beat, the signal for the Burgesses

On June 23, 1676 Nathaniel Bacon's volunteers massed outside the Assembly chambers, at the right end of the statehouse complex. Governor William Berkeley confronted the rebel as Thomas Mathew and other Burgesses looked on from the windows of the statehouse, but in the end Berkeley capitulated to Bacon's demand for a commission to lead provincial troops against the Indians. Berkeley's townhouse was on the left of the row and the statehouse on the right. (By Earl Mark, University of Virginia School of Architecture, in collaboration with the Jamestown Rediscovery Project and Johnson, Craven, and Gibson Architects, Charlottesville, Virginia. Courtesy of Virtual Jamestown)

to gather in their third-floor chamber. Berkeley closeted himself with the Council on the second floor.

Drawing some of his men up "to the very doore and windows of the state house," Bacon loudly demanded a commission as commander of Virginia's forces against the Indians. The Burgesses reminded Bacon that they, not Bacon's army, had been elected to legislate for the colony and insisted that "they had taken all possible care for carrying on the Indian Warr at the easiest charge that could be." The new bills redressed all of their constituents' complaints, and the Burgesses "desiered that for satisfaction of the people, what they had don might be publickly read."

"There [shall] be no bills read," replied Bacon.

The governor had had enough. Followed by his councilors, Berkeley erupted from the statehouse door, calling Bacon "a Rebell and a Traytor." Unbuttoning his shirt front, the apoplectic governor bared his breast.

"Here, Shoot me, foregod, fair Mark, Shoot," he cried, repeatedly.

"God damne his blood, I came for a Commission and a Comission I will have," swore Bacon.

Burgesses crowding the windows of their upstairs chamber saw Bacon "strutting betwixt Two files of men" with his left hand on his hip and "flinging his Right Arm every Way." Mathew clattered downstairs to join the gathering crowd, sticking with the sailors from his sloop for safety.

After several minutes Berkeley huffed off toward his townhouse at the other end of the statehouse row, followed by his councilors. An animated, furious Bacon turned to his men and ordered them to ready their weapons, then trailed after Berkeley with a detachment of soldiers.

Behind them, Bacon's men cocked their guns and took aim at the Burgesses crowding the statehouse windows, "repeating with Menacing Voices, 'We will have it, We will have itt.'" Bacon had instructed them to fire if he signaled them by drawing his sword, and as Mathew nervously watched Bacon following Berkeley in a "Paroxism of Phrentick fury" the rebel leader repeatedly grasped the hilt of his sword. Bacon seemed "delirious, and he was heard to say "Dam my Bloud, I'le Kill Governr Councill Assembly and all, and then Ile Sheath my Sword in my own heart's bloud."

After a half-minute of unbearable tension one of the Burgesses cracked, shaking out his handkerchief and waving it out the window while crying over and over again, "You shall have it, You shall have itt." Bacon's volunteers lowered their guns. This "Pacifick Handkercher" also calmed Bacon, who led his detachment back to the main body of the army on the nearby green. Berkeley, still furious, insisted that he would rather die than give Bacon a commission, but no one else felt quite so strongly. Under heavy pressure from the Council, Berkeley reluctantly agreed to sign one.[9]

As Bacon's men busied themselves with "drinking and domineereing" the townspeople after Friday's near-massacre, a mad scramble was on to control the aftermath of the Assembly's capitulation to Bacon. Berkeley and Bacon jostled over the wording of the commission and the number of blank officers' commissions the governor would sign, while Bacon and the Assembly argued over the Burgess's nearly completed legislation. On Saturday Bacon forced his way into the Burgesses' chamber and made them add a clause appointing him commander in chief to the declaration of war against the enemy Indians. He also pushed through additional laws pardoning all treasons committed since March 1 and barring from office two of Berkeley's prominent supporters.[10]

Berkeley spent much of the weekend writing a long, humiliating letter to Charles II praising the "manifestly sincere and Loyall" Bacon and excusing Bacon's followers for being "Somewhat irregular in the method of their Proceedings." At the same time, however, he secretly wrote a second letter to be hand-carried to England by his wife Frances. This letter told a completely different story, one in which he and his supporters feared for their lives at the hands of "young men that have not beene two Yeares in the Country." Bacon was trying to overturn the entire political order by appealing to the lowest ranks of society. The new governor, Berkeley concluded, should "come in a frigate"—that is, with military force.[11]

Bacon raced to get out his own version of events. He penned a competing letter to Crown officials explaining "our generall Aversion to Indians, as his Majesty's enemys." He also wrote to his father in England to help in spreading his version of events, and addressed the public in a "Plea for Opposing the Indians without the Governor's Order." Bacon was especially anxious to deny that his was a social revolution or even a rebellion against the king's authority. "No man could perceive in my manner, Estate, or manner of living" any sign of "levelling or rebellion." His was not a challenge to the existing order but rather its fulfillment: Governor Berkeley had failed in his responsibilities at a critical moment, and Bacon had merely allowed himself to be drafted "as the countries friend." Letters from Bacon's wife and friends backed up his account; meanwhile, Berkeley's friends were preparing to send off a sheaf of letters telling the governor's version of events.[12]

On Saturday night Mathew dined with his fellow Stafford County Burgess George Mason, the militia officer whose mistaken attack on the Susquehannock hunters' cabin the previous summer had caused so much mischief. Mason, drinking twice as much as Mathew that night, was worried that accepting a commission from Bacon would get him in trouble with Berkeley, while refusing it would anger Bacon. Mathew helpfully observed that if Mason and other gentlemen refused to serve, Bacon would be forced "to Appoint Commanders out of the Rabble," putting the "Estates of all in the Land" at risk of confiscation. Mason was persuaded, and after consulting the next day with "other Gentlemen in the same Circumstances," he decided to accept a commission from Bacon in order to prevent misrule by lesser men.

Mathew, hoping to avoid such entanglements himself, had already begged a member of the Council to press Berkeley to dissolve the Assembly. Eager to escape from "the Labyrinths and Snares of State Ambiguities," he was delighted to learn that the governor would soon be sending them home.

On Sunday evening many of the Burgesses gathered "to take our Leaves." Mathew joined them. Near sunset, Bacon entered the room carrying a sheaf of papers and asked, "which of these Gentlemen Shall I Intreat to write a few Words for me"? Most of the men, suddenly absorbed in their shoes or the cobwebs in the corners, appeared not to have heard the request. Richard Lawrence, however, pointed directly at Mathew and said "That Gentleman Writes very well." As Mathew tried to stammer out an excuse Bacon stood over him and said, "Pray Sir. Do me the Honour to write a Line for me." Mathew, shocked at his sudden misfortune, faced a dilemma. If he refused, he feared, "Stafford County would feel the smart of [Bacon's] Resentment." If he agreed, he would feel the governor's displeasure. But Bacon was looming over him, and Berkeley was not, and so Mathew sat up all night with Bacon filling in the blank officer's commissions signed by Berkeley. In the morning, after Bacon left Mathew to finish up on his own, Bacon's ardent supporter William Carver—a ship's captain—told poor Mathew that he was "in mighty favour" with Bacon. It was the last thing Mathew wanted to hear. His fondest wish was to go home and disappear from the view of the "Wise and the Rich" who were so "prone to Faction and Sedition."

Bacon and his army decamped early that morning, returning to their homes to defend against further Indian attacks and to plan the long-awaited campaign. The Burgesses, too, hastened homeward—none more eagerly than Mathew, who went directly from drafting Bacon's commissions to making his final preparations before setting sail. On his way out of town he spotted William Drummond, the former governor of North Carolina and one of Bacon's most ardent supporters. Mathew warned Drummond to be careful. Berkeley's rancor against him was well known, and it was rumored that "the Governour had put a brand upon him."

"I am in over Shoes," answered Drummond. "I will be in over Boots."[13]

· *Five* ·

# JAMESTOWN BURNING

Bacon left Jamestown after the June 1676 Assembly without declaring any specific plans for marching against the Indians. As the weeks passed puzzled Virginians began to suspect that his real targets were the Berkeley loyalists whose horses and weapons he was confiscating, and who he was imprisoning when they resisted his exactions. Finally, on July 15, Bacon called for a rendezvous at the falls of the James, where his thousand-man army would gather and be provisioned. The news that Bacon was at last ready for action quieted many of his critics. In a speech to the troops on the eve of their march he assured his men of his loyalty to king and country, taking an oath of allegiance to the king and urging the soldiers to do the same.

Once Bacon was safely away at the falls of the James the residents of Gloucester, a wealthy and populous county on the north side of the York River, sent a petition to Berkeley protesting that even though they had provided Bacon with everything he requested his men had acted "very rudely, both in words and actions, to the great disturbance of the Peace." Bacon's agent had personally held a colonel in the county militia at gunpoint and threatened to "pistoll him." He also had threatened to "ruine" a commissioner of the county court, swearing "with many fearfull Oaths, as God damne his blood, sink him, and rott him." The governor, they hoped, would help prevent "any more of these Outrages."

Berkeley read the Gloucester petition with growing eagerness, then scrawled his response at the bottom. The petition was "most willingly granted . . . to preserve his [Majesty's] loyall Subjects from all outrages and oppressions, to which they have been lately too much submitted by the Tyrany and Usurpation" of Bacon. Bacon's commission was "void in Law and Nature," no more legitimate "than if a Theif should take my purse, and make me own that I gave it him freely." Once again declaring Bacon a rebel, Berkeley called up the Gloucester and Essex county militias for service against both the Indians and the rebel army.

When Berkeley went to Gloucester County to address its assembled militia, however, he was bitterly disappointed. The militia and the county's leading men resented Bacon, yet few were willing to march against fellow Virginians "in this desperate conjuncture of time." They promised to fight if Bacon tried to overthrow the government, but so long as the rebel was attacking Indians they would leave him alone.

News of the governor's attempt to muster the Gloucester militia reached Bacon on the eve of the march against the Susquehannocks. Immediately he ordered drums and trumpets to interrupt the men's dinners so that he might address them. The governor was preparing to attack them, he reported. With Indians before them and Berkeley at their rear the army was threatened on two fronts, "like a candell att both ends." But Berkeley's supporters were cowards, Bacon assured his men, and they could be quickly dispersed.

"*Amen*," shouted the volunteers, "*Amen*."

Reasoning that it was better to "dye in the field, than be hang'd like [Rogues] or Perrish in the woods," they marched eastward next morning toward Jamestown. Along the way, several detachments peeled off to take over forts along the James and York rivers. The main body of Bacon's army arrived at Middle Plantation, a cluster of settlements at midpoint of the main road crossing the peninsula between the James and York rivers, on July 29. The volunteers set up camp just seven miles from Jamestown and even closer to Green Spring.

As the volunteers approached, Berkeley hastily packed what he could and abandoned Green Spring, fleeing across the Chesapeake Bay to the Eastern Shore. There, with forty prominent supporters and their families, he established his headquarters at John Custis's Arlington Plantation on Old Plantation Creek near the mouth of the Chesapeake Bay. There he awaited Bacon's next move.[1]

Bacon's critics were correct in supposing that he had not spent all of his time plotting the next Indian campaign. As Bacon's army settled in for their first full day at Middle Plantation their commander unveiled a defense of his own actions, a comprehensive indictment of the Berkeley faction, and a call for a convention to be held on August 3.

To defend himself from the "aspersion of Traitor and Rebell" Bacon released to the public his "Manifesto," a lengthy remonstrance to the king protesting Berkeley's misrule. Unless "vertue be a sin," he and his followers were no rebels. For what had they done, except to risk their lives in defending Virginia against Indian attacks? They had done so despite the interference of Berkeley and his "unworthy Favourites," a collection of "spounges" who despite their low birth and poor educations had risen to wealth on the backs of the people. Was it treason to speak of this travesty?

And what of the Indians? "Another main article of our Giult is our open and manifest aversion of all, not onely the Foreign but the protected and Darling Indians, this wee are informed is Rebellion of a deepe dye." Berkeley and his favorites defended neighbor Indians such as the Pamunkeys and Appomattoxes even though "they have bin for these Many years enemies to the King and Country, Robbers and Theeves and Invaders." Berkeley had even gone so far as to arm the Indians in order to enrich his favorites engaged in the Indian trade. Thus did the governor and the Indian traders "buy and sell our blood." Who, then, was the real traitor to the king and country?

Bacon answered this question in "The Declaration of the People, against Sir William Berkeley." Berkeley, Bacon concluded, "hath Traiterously attempted, violated and injured his Majesties' interest here." So had Berkeley's "wicked and Pernitious Councellors and Confederates," nineteen of whom Bacon listed by name. These "Traytors to the People" were given four days to surrender, after which all of their property would be seized. When captured they were to be brought to Middle Plantation.

"Most of the prime Gentlemen in these parts" answered Bacon's summons to gather at the Middle Plantation home of militia captain Otho Throp on August 3. Some of these men were so obviously reluctant that Bacon ordered them locked inside and guarded. At first he asked the planters only to prevent Berkeley from attacking his army from the rear while they were out fighting Indians, and to provide "insureance . . . not to have their throtes cut, when they should return hom, by those whoe had set them to worke."

Put this way, Bacon's demands did not seem unreasonable. Everyone agreed on the army's need for a "consistency of safety" during and after their campaign, and they drew up an oath to be taken against aiding Berkeley if he should try to attack Bacon. Bacon was pleased, but not satisfied. He wanted the oath-takers to promise to fight against Berkeley if the governor resisted the rebel army in any way, and even to fight against British troops sent from England until his cause could be accurately reported to the king. Every man in the room recoiled. They stood behind the oath of their own devising, but no one wanted to sign Bacon's version.

As the August sun rose higher and the heat and humidity mounted in the room, Bacon combined "threats and force and fear" with persuasion. He threatened to resign his commission. He pointed out that many men, including some of those present, had already been marked as rebels, and would be left unprotected if their fellow Virginians agreed merely to stand off to the side in the dispute with the governor. Only his stronger oath would protect them from retaliation.

At this critical moment one of the doors was unlocked to admit a panicked messenger from the York River fort, begging for immediate aid to the "grate many poore people" who had fled there for protection. Surprised and perplexed, Bacon wondered aloud "how could it posibl[y] be that the most conciderablest fortris in the countrey, should be in danger to be surprised by the Indians"? Because, replied the gunner, Berkeley had stripped the fort of arms and ammunition, "with which he was saled forth" out of the country.

Even Berkeley's supporters "did sta[g]ger" at this news. Suddenly Bacon's oath seemed easier to swallow. Seventy men, starting with Council member Thomas Swann, signed it. Another declaration, signed the next day, affirmed Bacon's authority and asked him to call a new assembly and establish a provisional government for Virginia. Bacon's oath was sent out to be taken by every freeman. Those who refused would have their names recorded and forwarded to General Bacon.

With that the conference broke up. Bacon directed his navy to track down Berkeley, and his army to march back to the falls of the James in pursuit of the Susquehannocks and Occaneechees. At last, Bacon was free to carry out "his favorite scheme of extirpating the Indians."[2]

Lord Baltimore had returned to London after Maryland's May Assembly, leaving Council member Thomas Notley as his deputy governor. In mid-August Notley met with the Council and with Maryland's Indian allies to discuss their situation. "There is a person called Collonel Bacon," he warned the Piscataways and Mattawomans, "who may perhaps come over into Maryland to annoy them." A similar warning was dispatched to London, informing Baltimore that there was "just cause to Suspect [Bacon] intends to embroyle the province in a Warr and that he will make the pursuit of the Pascattaway Indians his pretence to enter it."

In this atmosphere it seemed wise for the Council to assign a substantial guard to Governor Notley and to reorganize the command structure of the colony's militia. Major Henry Jowles, a twenty-six-year-old Protestant planter of French descent, replaced a less reliable officer in command of a Calvert County militia company, just north of St. Mary's City. Jowles and the other officers were directed to pay special attention to a neighborhood known as "the Clifts." The officers were told to be ready to march on an hour's notice.

The problem was that Clifts residents had been circulating a protest against Baltimore's rule, primarily at the instigation of William Davis, Giles Hasleham, and John Pate. In late August they "published" the protest to the militia company while it was mustered under Jowles's command, cocking and aiming their weapons at the major to prevent him from interfering as they read the document to the troops. Warrants went out for the leaders' arrest.

On September 3 Davis, still at large, convinced sixty men gathered at a Calvert County plantation "to extort from the Governour and Councell of this Province a grant of the contents of that paper." Notley's messengers arrived during the meeting bearing an offer to discuss their demands at the next meeting of the Assembly; in the meantime Notley would pardon everyone except Davies, who he promised "a free and legall tryall at the Provincial Court." Davis's response was to reject the governor's offers, form up his followers, and "march away with drummes beateing and Collours flying." Davis, Hasleham, and Pate escaped again.

Davis and Pate fled north up the Bay, crossing over the peninsula of the Eastern Shore to the Delaware River port of New

Castle before Baltimore's men caught up with them, brought them back to Maryland, and hanged them. Afterward Notley told Baltimore that never had a "Body" been "more repleat with Malignancy and Frenzy than our people were." It was fortunate that neither Davis nor Pate had possessed Bacon's influence and charisma. The only thing the rebels at the Clifts had lacked, Notley believed, was "a monstrous head to their monstrous body."[3]

Thomas Mathew stuck close to his plantation during these events, hoping to avoid any further entanglement with Indians, Marylanders, or Bacon's supporters. He avoided taking Bacon's oath, though he heard that bands of men were going house to house administering the oath and "Carrying away [as] Prisoners" those whom Bacon distrusted.

In mid-August Mathew was visited by a troop of horse under Major John Langston. Langston got right to the point: he brought "high Compliments" from General Bacon, who wanted Mathew to take command of his troops in northern Virginia. Although Langston was very insistent, Mathew politely refused. The veteran militia captain Giles Brent soon accepted the command, but Mathew nevertheless heard that Bacon "was mightily offended at my Evasions and threatened to Remember me."

Bacon had already "remembered" many Berkeley loyalists. His volunteer army had spent the first few days following the conference at Middle Plantation securing all of the fortifications on the James and York rivers. Then, on August 8, Bacon took possession of Berkeley's Green Spring plantation while his officers turned the homes of the other nineteen loyalists he had identified as "Traytors" into rebel garrisons.

Two days later the Surry County Court met across the river from Jamestown. The majority of the justices voted during that session to send provisions to Bacon, but at least one dissented: young Arthur Allen, only twenty-four years old but already the master of a magnificent three-story brick mansion and a large plantation, a member of the local vestry, and a county surveyor. Allen could see where this affair was headed. At the conclusion of the court session he went home, hid his silver, and awaited the return of William Berkeley.[4]

At Green Spring Bacon was learning that rumors, which usually worked to his advantage, could also have the opposite effect. "Most of his forces," people were saying, wasted their time "in revelling and drinkeing" at the looted homes of loyalists, even as Indian attacks penetrated to within a few miles of Jamestown. Only a successful march against the Indians would quiet fears that this ragtag army was merely a "rebellion of the Vulgar." So, after sending out an order to hold elections for a new assembly, Bacon finally led his army toward the falls of the James in mid-August.

The road passed near the Pamunkeys' settlements. Cocka-coeske's scouts doubtless watched and followed as the volunteers headed upriver. She knew, as well, when Bacon turned around almost immediately after reaching the falls and doubled back toward the York River to meet up with hundreds of northern Virginia troops under Giles Brent. The Susquehanocks and Occaneechees, it was evident, were beyond Bacon's reach, but not so the Pamunkeys and other nations within the Virginia settlements.

Heavy rains delayed Bacon and Brent from attacking the Pamunkeys, giving Cockacoeske time to lead her nation into hiding in the thick woods and swamps north of the York River. Bacon could not find them. Soon the English were reduced to marching "att randome" along likely looking paths. When they finally did stumble upon Cockacoeske's camp on a sandy point projecting into a swamp, they made so much noise in their approach that most of the Pamunkeys escaped. Bacon's army looted her camp and captured a small child and an old woman who Bacon hoped would guide him to Cockacoeske. Instead the woman led them away from Cockacoeske. When Bacon finally discovered the trick a day and a half later, he ordered his men to kill her. Leaving the old woman's corpse sprawled across the path, they retraced their steps to the camp and resumed their wanderings.

With the September 4 Assembly approaching, the volunteers had killed or captured barely a half-dozen Indians. The army was "Murmuringe, Impatient, hunger-starv'd, dissatisfied." Heavy rains soaked their clothing, weighed down their packs, and mired their feet in mud. It seemed as if Bacon had not had "one dry day in all his Marches to and fro in the Forrest," even though elsewhere in Virginia the summer was so dry that corn and tobacco were withering in the fields. Tales of this misery spread even to the Potomac, where Mathew heard that the people were blaming the miserable combination of drought and drenching rains on "the *Pawawings*, i.e. the Sorceries of the Indians." Bacon had little choice but to send most of his army away, including all of Brent's Northern Neck men. The army broke camp before dawn the next morning, with most men marching homeward while 136 men under Bacon continued to hunt Indians.

Bacon stumbled upon the Pamunkey camp just three hours later.

The Pamunkeys scattered before Bacon's charging men, leaving behind most of their possessions as they dived into the thickets, ducked behind trees, and crawled under a mass of grape vines. Shots and cries rang out and English voices rose as they ransacked the camp for mats, baskets, cloth, beads, skins, and furs. At last trumpets sounded to call back the attackers with their captives, forty-five in all. Cockacoeske decided to surrender herself. As she returned to the camp, however, she stumbled upon the mangled body of a Pamunkey woman, "which struck such terror in the Queen, that fearinge their cruelty by that gastly example, she went on her first intended way into the wild woods."

Bacon, refreshed and encouraged, decided to continue his search for Indians even as the date for the new Assembly he had called came and went. Cockacoeske, "lost and missinge from her own people," survived for two weeks on scraps of small game brought her by a ten-year-old boy. Only when she was about to die from starvation did she emerge from the woods and surrender to the English. The other Pamunkey prisoners, it was later revealed, were sold into slavery.[5]

Berkeley was easier to hunt down than Cockacoeske, although it took several weeks to sift through the conflicting rumors about his whereabouts. He had sailed for London or the West Indies, some said, or he might be hiding aboard a ship still anchored near Jamestown. Finding him was the task of an amphibious force under the command of a disgruntled customs collector, Giles Bland, and the retired ship's captain William Carver, who a month earlier had tried and failed to recruit Thomas Mathew as an officer in the volunteer army.

On August 1, 300 volunteers under Carver and Bland took possession of several ships anchored in the James River. They were especially eager to capture Captain Christopher Evelyn's *Rebecca* because Berkeley and some of his leading supporters were rumored to be aboard. But someone tipped off Evelyn, and the *Rebecca* slipped away. The crew of another ship, also named *Rebecca*, fired against the raiders but was soon taken. The captain, Thomas Larrimore, was briefly imprisoned, then allowed to be the master of his old ship under the command of Carver and Bland. Guns from the Jamestown fort were transferred to the *Rebecca*, which became the mainstay of Bacon's eight-ship navy.

Carver and Bland spent the next few weeks patrolling the rivers, suppressing the governor's supporters and spreading the message of the "Manifesto" and "Declaration of the People." Somewhere along the way they picked up Berkeley's trail, discovering that the governor, far from being gone for London, was still within their grasp across the Bay at John Custis's Arlington Plantation. In the last days of August the *Rebecca* and another, smaller ship under the command of Carver and Bland appeared off Rose Mary Point, a rounded peninsula on the south side of Old Plantation Creek. Leaving Bland anchored in the Bay aboard the *Rebecca* along with forty soldiers, seventy sailors, and former captain Thomas Larrimore, Carver brought 160 men ashore in the smaller vessel, negotiating the short stretch of shoals and small islands at the creek's mouth and anchoring before Arlington Plantation. Berkeley had no choice but to deploy his guard to keep Carver at bay while awaiting some way to evade Carver's trap.

Most of the marines remained aboard the *Pinnace* while Carver rowed ashore and began negotiations with the governor. Berkeley stretched out the talks for hours while probing for some advantage; Carver, confident that Berkeley's guard would sooner or later become less vigilant, was happy to play along. At some point in the evening a contrary wind came up, making it impossible for the pinnace to sail back to the larger *Rebecca*. The two men continued talking into the night.

Berkeley found his opening near midnight, when a secret message from the *Rebecca's* Master Larrimore slipped through Carver's lines. Before the ship's capture Larrimore and his crew had backed the governor; now, with Carver's contingent of 160 men gone, the *Rebecca's* original crew outnumbered the men left behind with Bland. If Berkeley would send men out to the *Rebecca*, Larrimore offered, his men would help retake the ship.

When dawn broke the loyalist boarding party could clearly be seen in their small passenger boat making for the mouth of Plantation Creek and the *Rebecca* beyond. The loyalists clambered through the gun ports, conveniently left open by Larrimore, even before Bland knew they were there. The loyalists captured the ship so quickly that when Carver arrived with reinforcements they already lined the rail, aiming their muskets down at the rebel pursuers. Carver had no choice but to surrender. The men left behind on Carver's pinnace, caught as they were between the governor's guard ashore and the *Rebecca* at sea, also surrendered.

William Carver was hanged at Accomack several days later. Even as his limp body swayed at the end of a noose, Larrimore was out on the Bay gathering a navy. Already he had captured the last of Carver's four vessels, and within a few more days Larrimore had acquired at least ten ships as loyalists rallied to the governor's side. Suddenly, Berkeley controlled the Chesapeake Bay and the rivers. It was time to sail for Jamestown and to begin the reconquest of Virginia.[6]

The first of Berkeley's ships appeared off the eastern end of Jamestown Island on the evening of September 7. The tide and wind turned against the loyalist navy, forcing the larger ships to anchor just downstream from the island while they awaited the next day's incoming tide and upriver breezes. The smaller, more maneuverable sloops pressed on, working up the eddies close to shore until they reached the western tip of the island, just off the statehouse and the fort. Nearly a thousand rebels under the command of Thomas Hanford occupied the town.

That evening Berkeley sent ashore a proclamation offering a pardon to everyone except Bacon, Drummond, and Lawrence. Some of the town's defenders wanted to accept. Others feared that the governor would not keep his word and that they would "meet with som after-claps of revenge." Unwilling either to surrender or to stand and fight, they decided instead to desert Jamestown during the night, scattering to their homes or rejoining Bacon's army before the loyalists could cut off their escape from the island. Berkeley was astonished to discover, the next morning, that the rebels had abandoned the capital without a fight. He imagined with relish Bacon's reaction upon learning of "our smal numbers when we landed." Surely, he thought, the rebel leader would swear "a Thousand of his execrable oaths"!

Berkeley was rowed into Jamestown near midday, the red tiled roof of his townhouse visible at the end of statehouse row. Stepping ashore he knelt and "rendred thanks unto God for his safe arrival," then set to work. Bacon, he assumed, would soon return. The island's defenses, built with an eye to guarding against attacks by sea, would have to be reconfigured, and quickly, to ward off an army approaching by land.[7]

Bacon was not in peak form when news of Berkeley's return reached his encampment at the head of the York River. Nearly all of his men, exhausted from weeks of chasing through swamps, had gone home. Hansford brought only a few soldiers from Jamestown. Altogether Bacon could muster only about 150 men, some of whom had deployed to guard the Pamunkey captives.

None of this gave Bacon pause. Calling together his small band, he assured them that they held the advantage. While they marched toward Jamestown, displaying their Indian prisoners as reminders of their recent triumph, Berkeley's men would doubtless be cowering at the rebels' approach. "You have the Prayers and well wishes of all the People in Virginia," he insisted, while the governor's men "are loaded with their curses." What Bacon did not say, and perhaps did not need to, was that if captured they would hang. Their situation was so desperate, in fact, that Bacon now "proclam'd liberty to all Servants and Negros" who joined his army.

Bacon launched his assault on September 13, briefly skirmishing with mounted loyalists before riding onto the beach before the capital's defenses. Bacon's men spent the night "in fallinge of trees, cuttinge of Bushes and throwinge up of earth," digging mostly by hand (or squabbling over their two axes and two spades) as they toiled by the light of the moon.

On his return from exile on the Eastern Shore William Berkeley could see his townhouse, at the west end of the statehouse complex, from the deck of his ship. When Berkeley landed he knelt and "rendred thanks unto God." (Image by Earl Mark, University of Virginia, in collaboration with the Jamestown Rediscovery Project and with Johnson, Craven, and Gibson Architects, Charlottesville, Virginia. Courtesy of Virtual Jamestown)

While most of Bacon's men dug trenches, others went looking for loyalist women. Next morning, Berkeley's gunners were astonished to see "all of the prime mens wives, whose Husbands were with the Governour," standing atop the rebels' breastworks, conspicuously visible in their white aprons. To the chagrin of the town's defenders their "innocent and harmless Wives" were lined up as "a white garde to the Divill." Unable to attack without first being "obliged to dart there wepons through there wives brest,"

the loyalists watched helplessly as Bacon's men finished their fortifications, releasing the women only after their defenses were
ready.

With the women out of harm's way, the governor nearly emptied out the town in an all-out attempt to dislodge Bacon. Arthur
Allen, the young Surry County planter who had refused to vote
to send supplies to Bacon, led the way. Behind him at least 600
men marched shoulder to shoulder, with those suspected of
being the least committed to the loyalist cause being forced into
the front ranks. These were easy targets for Bacon's men, who
were screened from view by heaps of brush and protected from
lucky shots by trenches and earthworks. The first volleys from the
trenches scattered the lukewarm soldiers in the loyalist front
lines. The remainder quickly joined them, abandoning weapons,
their drum, and even the bodies of the fallen in their haste. In the
wake of the loyalists' humiliation it was all Bacon could do to
prevent his men from overextending themselves by storming the
town's fortifications.

Yet Bacon's situation remained perilous. While the loyalists
rested in townhouses, tents, or belowdecks on the ships anchored
off Jamestown, Bacon and his men, pinned down most of the
time in muddy, open-air trenches, could neither shelter themselves from the wet and damp nor dry off properly between rain
showers. In the close, crowded quarters, infestations of lice spread
from soldier to soldier.[8]

Even as the two sides dug into their positions at Jamestown, the
rest of Virginia remained in turmoil. Consider the case of Arthur
Allen. On the same day that he led the failed loyalist assault on

Bacon's trenches, his overseer John Finley was captured by a detachment of Baconites across the James in Surrey County. Shortly afterward Allen led a provisioning raid against one of his own southside neighbors, missing Finley and his captors by only a day. Allen delivered his haul of bread and cheese to Jamestown, then returned to Surry County to requisition horses from his neighbors—while just a few miles away, yet another 300 rebels under William Rookman descended upon the Allen mansion. Allen's aged mother could only stand by and watch as the rebels helped themselves to the liquor, slaughtered the livestock, trampled the crops in the fields, and made the magnificent mansion their headquarters in Surry County.[9]

The civil war had become so chaotic that many of the colony's ordinary folk must have felt like sheep being endlessly driven back and forth. The rumors of Indian attacks seemed unending, and it was almost impossible to know which ones were true. The governor came and went from Jamestown, sometimes threatening the noose and sometimes capitulating to the rebels. Bacon recruited men to fight the Indians but then diverted them to battle the loyalists. Each leader proclaimed loyalty to the king and declared the other a traitor. The losers were likely to hang when the game of musical chairs finally stopped. Small wonder that there was so much changing of sides, that so many people were anxious to avoid lining up under either of these two uncertain standards.

In the midst of this chaotic swirl, the fragile balance of power shifted again. On the northern frontier, where Giles Brent led Bacon's forces, news that Berkeley had occupied Jamestown caused Brent to change sides. Only a few weeks after having accompanied Bacon on his hunt for the Pamunkeys, Brent now gathered hundreds of men to race southward to break Bacon's siege of the capital city.

Jamestown's loyalist defenders, however, had heard nothing of Brent's decision to help them; in contrast, they could see that reinforcements were coming into Bacon's camp and that his men were digging in for a long siege. On September 17, two days after Allen's failed sally, Bacon brought up three large guns and installed them while parading some of his Indian captives on the ramparts—a timely reminder to any fence-sitters of the difference between his policy of Indian extermination and of Berkeley's insistence on maintaining the colony's Native alliances. After the guns had been installed behind the screen of Pamunkey captives, Bacon shelled the governor's ships until they withdrew from their positions. He fired upon Jamestown's fortifications as well, trying to open a breach in the palisade in preparation for an assault on the town. Although the defenders still controlled the Bay and the rivers, their confidence was badly shaken. Loyalist officers began to lose control over their men.

Berkeley did his best to shore up morale. On September 17 he spent the entire day riding between outposts encouraging his troops. Exhausted but satisfied that he had "left them al ful of courage," he turned in before sundown. Already, however, a rumor was racing through the ranks that hundreds of Bacon's men had landed behind the town's fortifications. No sooner had Berkeley lain down to rest than several officers came to his townhouse to report that some of the soldiers were mutinying and running away. Berkeley threw on his clothes, gathered forty men, and raced to the place where Bacon's landing was supposed to have taken place. There was no one there, and no sign in the wet ground that there had been a landing. Exasperated, Berkeley lectured his officers and went back to bed.

Early the next morning, before Berkeley could resume his rounds, more officers came to the townhouse and urged him to abandon Jamestown. Berkeley objected that the loyalist cause would lose its credibility if they left, and that Bacon's long-suffering men were likely to mutiny themselves if the siege dragged on much longer. Nothing worked. Even a last-ditch appeal to honor and manhood left the officers unmoved. Berkeley, disgusted, finally demanded that they sign a statement that they, and not he, had insisted on "the necessity of my dishonorable quitting the place."

Berkeley pocketed the officers' statement and ordered the town evacuated. That night, under cover of darkness, Jamestown's defenders slipped out to their ships, weighed anchor, and let the outgoing tide silently carry them downriver. Bacon's army occupied the town early next morning.

News of Brent's approach arrived later that day. Bacon hurriedly consulted with his officers over their dilemma: holding on to Jamestown while loyalist ships controlled the river and Brent's army occupied the trenches built by Bacon's men would be almost impossible, but allowing Berkeley to recapture Jamestown was unthinkable.

Bacon did not flinch. Later that night he ordered his men to set fire to the town so that "the [Rogues] shoud harbor no more there." Lawrence relayed the command, but the men "abhorred such Barbarity" and refused to obey. Lawrence himself had to take the lead. Starting with his own house and tavern he "became the executioner, and fired the Houses with his own Hands."

The Ruins of the Brick Church Tower at Jamestown. (Courtesy of Preservation Virginia)

Drummond joined in, burning down his own home as well. Soon their soldiers picked up brands too, torching more homes, the statehouse complex, warehouses, taverns, and even the old brick church.

Berkeley and the loyalist refugees had not gone far since abandoning the town that morning. Uncertain as to their next move, they merely allowed the current to carry them a short way downstream to the lower end of Jamestown Island, then set their anchors. When darkness fell upon the river they were still there, a mere three miles from the town. That night, from the deck of his ship, Governor Berkeley helplessly watched the fiery glow of Jamestown burning.[10]

· *Six* ·

# "The Uproars of Virginia Have Been Stupendious"

Bacon lingered at Green Spring for several days after the destruction of Jamestown, then led his men over the peninsula between the James and York rivers on his way to confront Giles Brent's advancing northern army. Once across the York he paused in Gloucester County to address the local militia. The stories Bacon had heard made it seem as if the militia had rejected Berkeley altogether at the time of the Gloucester petition, so he was surprised when the Gloucester men resisted taking the pro-Bacon oath that had been circulating since early August. But with Brent's army fast approaching, Bacon decided to ride north first and deal with Gloucester later.

It didn't take long. To the surprise of many, Brent's army disintegrated before a shot was fired. As one cynic put it, "haveing heard that Bacon had beate the Governour out o'th Towne they began to be afeared (if they should com with in his reach) that he might beat them out of their lives, and so resolved not to come near him."

Within days Bacon was back in Gloucester County to settle his differences. "One Mr. Cole," recalled one observer, "offered the sence of all the Gloster men, there present: which was sum'd up in their desires, not to have the oath imposed upon them, but to be indulged in the benifitt of Neutralitie." When a local minister, James Wading, encouraged the men to refuse the oath, Bacon had him arrested. It was Wading's job, Bacon said, "to preach in the Church, not in the Camp." Cowed if not persuaded, the Gloucester men subscribed to the oath.[1]

The intimidation of the Gloucester populace did not end with Bacon's Oath. House Speaker Augustine Warner's plantation lay at a landing on the pleasant, narrow Severn River. Warner, who was away with Berkeley on the Eastern Shore, had left his twenty-seven-year-old relative and overseer John Townley in charge at Warner Hall. Anticipating trouble, Townley took an inventory of the plantation's household goods in late September 1676 and put as much as possible under lock and key.

No sooner had Townley completed the inventory than Nathaniel Bacon and William Byrd arrived at the head of 200 horse and foot soldiers. Bacon, Townley later testified, confiscated the keys to the storerooms and handed them over to Byrd. Byrd parceled out Warner's possessions to his men, keeping a sword and shoulder belt for himself and reserving the finest silks and linens for Bacon.

Bacon and Byrd did not stay long, but Townley was convinced that they would return. He quickly organized the Warner household, supervising servants and slaves as they carried the remaining household goods across the gently sloping field between Warner Hall and the Severn River to a waiting ship. Checking the goods against his recent inventory Townley calculated the losses at £845, about as much as Warner might expect to make from the labor of forty servants and slaves in a year.[2]

On the night that Berkeley was forced to abandon Jamestown, Captain Robert Morris piloted the 267-ton *Young Prince* into the Chesapeake Bay at the end of a long passage from England. The next afternoon Morris anchored inside the mouth of the James, where he met with another recently arrived ship, the *Richard and Elizabeth* under Nicholas Prynne, and learned what had happened since his last visit. The two captains decided to sail to Jamestown and put themselves at the governor's disposal. They started upriver next morning, but a strong north wind and heavy rain drove them back to anchor. After another day of bad weather, a sloop from upstream brought news that Berkeley had quit Jamestown and the rebels had put it to the torch. Over the next few days the northerly wind kept Morris and Prynne pinned to their anchorage and pushed a steady stream of shipping downstream, including, on September 27, William Berkeley's ship. Delighted to have naval support, Berkeley organized the captains into two squadrons: one under Thomas Gardiner to carry the governor back to his Eastern Shore refuge before returning to attack rebel positions on the York River, and the other, under Morris, to patrol the James River. Morris wasted no time, sailing the next morning to intercept enemy shipping and support loyalists fighting mostly on the south side of the James.

Each night Morris sat down to write (or dictate) his journal for the day in a clean, tidy script that was at odds with the disorder of events. He evacuated and landed small numbers of loyalist troops as needed and kept the river clear of enemy boats and ships, but the patrols could catch only glimpses of what was going on ashore. Clearly the Baconites under Thomas Hansford controlled much of the territory on either side of the river. In addition, Bacon's fellow Henrico County Burgess James Crews was marching downriver and driving loyalists out before him. On October 4 Morris and Prynne entertained rebel emissaries who wished to recruit them to the other side, from which they were able to infer that Bacon was trying to establish normal governmental functions. By October 21, however, even this trickle of information had tapered off. Morris was reduced to terse journal entries recording only the weather.

The little loyalist navy was too small to patrol the colony's other rivers, leaving Berkeley even more in the dark about the rebellion in the northern counties where it had begun. Yet even if he had known more it would have been difficult to detect a pattern in the shifting events of that autumn. Brent's army marched back and forth over the northern peninsulas, sometimes in Bacon's service and sometimes in Berkeley's. The regular workings of local government lapsed: at least one county court did not meet for nearly a year. Armed men rode about administering Bacon's oath, a minister was expelled from his church by the rebels, and numerous loyalists were imprisoned. Yet not all went in favor of the rebels; some said that there was also a loyalist uprising against the Baconites on the Northern Neck.[3]

At some moment during the fall, perhaps while huddling in a crowded, damp trench before Jamestown, Nathaniel Bacon began scratching at the body lice crawling under his clothing and feeding on his blood. Soon such "Swarmes of Vermine . . . bred in his body" that he had to burn his clothing every time he changed. At least one of the lice had previously fed upon the blood of someone carrying the bacterium *Rickettsia prowazekii*, which then bred in the louse's gut until Bacon scratched the louse's bite, crushing the host and grinding its infected feces into the small wound it had made in his flesh. A week or two later Bacon fell ill with a crushing headache and other flu-like symptoms and was bedridden in the Gloucester County home of Major Thomas Pate with a full-blown case of typhus. To this was added a "bloody flux" that turned his bowels inside out. By mid-October Bacon was delirious, "very much dissatisfied in mind, enquiring over and anon after the arrival of the frigatts and forces" that he expected soon from England. Even a visit from the Reverend Wading, released from his imprisonment in the controversy over Bacon's oath, gave the general no relief. Nathaniel Bacon died on October 26, 1676, a day recorded by Captain Morris as one of "raney misty weather."

As Thomas Mathew heard the tale, Bacon's closest advisors spirited away the corpse and buried it in a secret place so that his bones could not "be Exposed on a Gibbet as was purpos'd." In the absence of a body that might be memorialized or condemned, Virginians turned to verse. "Bacons Epitaph" lamented his death in forty-four lines, beginning with the wail

> Death why soe crewill! what, no other way
> To manifest thy splleene, but thus to slay
> Our hopes of safety; liberty, our all
> Which, through thy tyranny, with him must fall

To which a loyalist poet fired back in forty-eight lines,

> Whether to Ceaser was he Friend or Foe?
> Pox take such Ignorance, do you not know?
> Can he be Friend to Ceaser, that shall bring
> The Arms of Hell, to fight against the King?

But Berkeley's favorite epitaph, only two lines long, came from the pen—or so he said—of "an honest minister":

> Bacon is Dead I am sorry at my hart
> that Lice and flux should take the hangmans part.[4]

News of the tumult in Virginia had begun trickling into London during the spring, and by late June Crown officials were becoming very concerned that it might pose a threat to "the Interests of State at home and abroad." Most distressingly, it imperiled the estimated £100,000 of annual revenue from the tobacco excise that Charles II stood to lose. Such a loss would have to be made up by asking Parliament for more subsidies, and they would doubtless exact heavy political concessions in return. Anxious to bring order to the colony, the king's Privy Council voted to send a small mountain of hand grenades, guns, powder, and shot to put down the rebellion and began to consider the possibility of sending troops to the colony. Charles II ordered a warship sent to Virginia as soon as better information on the situation could be obtained, and the secretary of the navy was ordered to assemble a naval force.

Four months later the king was still finding it difficult to piece together a coherent picture. Charles II's Cabinet Council prepared for its October 1 meeting by reading the spate of competing reports, letters, and declarations dispatched from Virginia at the end of the June Assembly, including Bacon's "Declaration of the People" and "Manifesto" of late July, accounts of the Middle Plantation convention in early August, and a personal plea for leniency from the rebel's father Thomas Bacon.

Rather less information had come in from loyalists, which was interpreted in London as an indication that the rebels controlled Virginia. Charles signed a series of directives for suppressing the rebellion and addressing popular grievances, and ordered 1,000 soldiers under Colonel Herbert Jeffreys transported to Virginia in a fleet commanded by Sir John Berry. The two commanders, joined by Frances Moryson, Virginia's lobbyist in England, were commissioned to investigate the disturbances.

In mid-October papers finally arrived with the governor's side of the story. These clarified matters for Charles, who proclaimed that Bacon had "in a Traiterous and Rebellious manner levyed War . . . against the Kings most Excellent Majesty." The king offered a large reward for Bacon's capture and extended amnesty to his followers if they surrendered within twenty days of the proclamation's publication in Virginia. The king signed the document on October 27, unaware that Bacon had died just a few hours earlier.

The warship *Bristol* had been poised to leave since late August, but the preparations to send troops were time-consuming and expensive and the information on events in Virginia remained so sketchy that it seemed best to hold her back. On November 14, however, the master of a ship from Virginia told Charles of Berkeley's late-August capture of the *Rebecca*. Was Virginia now fully engulfed in a civil war? "The uproars of Virginia have been so Stupendious," Secretary of State Henry Coventry wrote the following day, "That in any Age but ours that hath been accustomed to Prodigies they would hardly find belief." Charles ordered the commissioners and troops to leave for America as soon as possible. The *Bristol*, carrying Berry, Moryson, and seventy soldiers, sailed on November 19. Colonel Jeffreys scrambled to depart with the rest of the fleet, sailing into the stormy North Atlantic on December 3.[5]

Bacon was dead, but the rebellion did not die with him. Indeed, the fiercest fighting was yet to come, and the rebels' politics became more radical after their leader went to his secret grave.

Bacon left behind a well-established command structure and network of garrisons. William Rookin's detachment at Arthur Allen's home was just one of four garrisons on the south side of the James, while on the other side of the river 100 rebels occupied Berkeley's Green Spring plantation. The York River was even more heavily defended, with four garrisons in Gloucester County alone. On the south bank soldiers were ensconced at the "Brick House" garrison and, several miles downstream, at the home of loyalist Council member Nathaniel Bacon. Twin garrisons at Tindall's Point and at Colonel George Reade's confiscated home directly across the river from Tindall's Point guarded the approach from the Bay.

Most of the commanders at these garrisons were well known to Virginians. Richard Lawrence, who according to many was the puppet master behind Bacon's Rebellion, was in excellent health at the Brick House garrison. So was former North Carolina governor William Drummond. Thomas Hansford took over the highly exposed position at Colonel Reade's, and William Byrd was across the York at Tindall's Point. James Crews commanded one of the James River garrisons.

At the head of the rebellion, however, was a newcomer to Virginia. Joseph Ingram had arrived only in 1674 but had quickly established himself by marrying a wealthy widow and entering into a business partnership with fellow planter Gregory Walklate. Ingram was already being spoken of as a leading rebel as early as the closing of the June Assembly. With Bacon's death he emerged as "Generall of all the forces," with Walklate as his second in command. Ingram established his headquarters at Thomas Pate's Gloucester County plantation (where Bacon had died) and at West Point, which commanded a strategic position at the mouths of two smaller rivers that combined to form the York.

Ingram was a slightly mysterious and shady character, at least in the eyes of his loyalist opponents. "Joseph Ingram," some said, was not his real name. Perhaps, they insinuated, it was the alias of a man who had come to Virginia to escape hanging in England? "It is said," wrote a York planter, "that he could dance well upon a rope." Bacon had been the "Lion," but Ingram was "the Ape," or "the Milksop," or "Tit mouse," or "the Peacock." The nicest thing any of the governor's supporters had to say was that Ingram was a tidy, overly fussy and particular man.[6]

The people who said such unflattering things, however, committed their words to paper only when safely within loyalist territory. Ingram's soldiers and fellow officers, meanwhile, spoke through their actions. They accepted him as Bacon's successor.

By the time he learned of Bacon's death Berkeley felt a bit like Noah: he had been "shut up in the Arke" of his Eastern Shore retreat for weeks and was eager to discover if "the Delluge was any whit abated, and whether any dry-ground emerg'd."[7]

It had, but only in patches. The weather improved on the evening of Bacon's death, and Morris resumed his patrols along the lower James the next morning. His blockade bottled up the rebels within the river, but it neither prevented them from scurrying back and forth across the James nor dislodged them from their positions ashore. His first priority was to control shipping along the James, so he was not always free to exploit weaknesses in the rebels' defenses.

Morris's patience paid off only slowly, and in small increments. In early November, for example, John Gatlin, commander of one of the Southside garrisons, began negotiations to change sides. By the end of the month he had surrendered. Still, most of the Southside remained in rebel hands, and Morris's raids were inconclusive at best. A typical foray in December killed fifteen rebels, but fifteen loyalists also died in the attack. On Christmas Eve, more than three months into Morris's blockade, "the rogues on Shore" felt spirited enough to taunt the ship-bound loyalists over their inability to go ashore.[8]

The loyalists made better progress along the York River. Robert Beverley, a wealthy Rappahannock River planter and the clerk of the Assembly, had been listed by Bacon as one of the twenty "traytors" to the people. After the evacuation of Jamestown Beverley joined Berkeley on the Eastern Shore. When news arrived that Bacon was dead Berkeley dispatched Beverley and a landing force he had gathered to strike at rebel positions on the York River. Sailing across Chesapeake Bay and up the York, Beverley first encountered the rebel garrisons at Tindall's Point and directly across the river at Colonel George Reade's. These positions commanded fine views downriver and would be very difficult to take by surprise—especially if their commanders had the wits to consult a tide table to determine when loyalist ships would be most likely to sail upriver.

Yet somehow Hansford was caught completely by surprise on the morning of November 7. His men failed to notice the loyalists sailing upriver, rowing ashore, and climbing the hill to Reade's mansion. Hansford was sound asleep when the raiders broke into his room. Perhaps, as some said, he was tired and distracted because he had "forsaken the Capitole of Mars"—war—"to pay his oblations in the Temple of Venus"—sex. Hansford's men were also caught napping, and before reinforcements could arrive Beverley had carried off twenty prisoners, back across the Bay to Accomack, where they were immediately court-martialed.[9]

Sentenced to die, Hansford asked only to "be shot like a Soulder, and not to be hang'd like a dog." The charge, however, was treason, and the punishment for that was hanging. Hansford used what little time remained to him "by repentance and contrition for all his Sinns . . . excepting his Rebellion, which he would not acknowledg."

Bouyed by his victory, Beverley returned directly to the York without even waiting to see Hansford's hanging. There he scored a series of successful quick raids, returning each time to Accomack with more prisoners and condemned men to hang or await their fates in confinement on the Eastern Shore. By late December, Berkeley had 100 prisoners at Accomack.

Yet Beverley no more controlled the land along the York than Morris did along the James, and he even suffered some reversals.

In a mid-November raid 120 men under Hubert Farrill raided the rebel garrison at the home of Nathaniel Bacon the elder. A thirty-man rebel guard under Major Whaley defended the garrison. Farrill's men rowed quietly across the river from the governor's ship in predawn darkness, and with Councilor Bacon as their guide sneaked uphill from the landing. Their orders were to hold their fire until they reached the house, but when a sentry challenged them several loyalists discharged their muskets. Whaley scrambled to pull together his defenders, positioning some men in Bacon's house and others along the approaches to the garrison. With no way of knowing who the shadowy figures in the darkness were, the loyalists "fired one upon the other, giveing the Bullits leave to grope there owne way in the dark." One hit Farrill in the groin. The attackers fled, leaving behind Farrill's corpse and abandoning several laggards who became Whaley's prisoners.

The rebels' weakest link, potentially, was Gloucester County, whose militia had repeatedly rejected Berkeley's and Bacon's overtures alike. While the governor's ships continued to lock down rebel traffic on the York, Berkeley tried again to sway Gloucester to his side—this time with some success. Major Lawrence Smith agreed to muster the county's militia at Thomas Pate's house while the rebel commander Ingram was away, and then convinced 600 men to ride north against rebels in Middlesex County. Ingram quickly dispatched horsemen under Walklate to intercept them, and led another party to retake Gloucester County in Smith's absence. Smith countered by sending some of his men back to meet Ingram and leading others forward toward Middlesex County. But Walklate easily scattered Smith's northbound force, and Ingram "very nimbly" recaptured Pate's house. The retreating

Gloucester loyalists flew so quickly back to Pate's that they momentarily caught Ingram by surprise. Had Smith's men already defeated Walklate, Ingram wondered, and then raced back to Pate's to attack him? Ingram soon realized, however, that the Gloucester men "did not weare (in there faces) the Countinances of Conquerers." Instead of exploiting their momentary advantage Smith's men stood "like a Company of Sheep, with the knife at there throtes, and never so much as offer to Bleat." It was a great gift to Ingram, this "tame surrender" of Gloucester County's loyalists.[10]

Although Maryland's governor and Council had successfully put down September's Affair at the Clifts, they were still struggling to combat unrest that at any moment might merge with the armed rebellion in Virginia. At a new session in early December the councilors expressed their amazement at the ingratitude of Marylanders "who have bin so farre blinded by the Spetious pretences of some desperate and ill Affected persons as to runn out into an Actuall Rebellion."

Berkeley's appeasement of the Baconites had obviously not worked, so Notley and the Council took a harder line. They were prepared, they warned, to "by the sword of Justice lopp off such rotten members as doe Endanger the whole." Those who complained about high taxes would have to pay them anyway, because the Susquehannock War had to be paid for. So too would the cost of suppressing the rebellion at the Clifts, which had served only to increase the province's debt. Maryland's Baconites, the councilors urged, must work through the elected Assembly in the future so that there would "be noe further need of Expensive forces" to quell a rebellion.

As Notley saw it, Virginia's insurrection and Maryland's unrest were fomented by the same people as part of a single cause. Therefore, he ordered, Marylanders were forbidden to trade with Virginians until the rebellion there was over: not for food, not for tobacco, and certainly not for arms or ammunition. Those who did would be prosecuted as "Aiders Assisters and Abettors of those that have actually Levyed Warr in Virginia against Our Soveraigne Lord the King."[11]

Captain Thomas Grantham sailed regularly to Virginia during these years. He had commanded one of the merchant vessels attacked by the Dutch at the mouth of the James in 1673. In the winter of 1673–1674 he led the London tobacco fleet over (with Joseph Ingram as a passenger, as it happened). As usual Grantham stayed in Virginia for months, negotiating with planters to load their enormous hogsheads of tobacco for passage home. When visiting Jamestown, he usually stayed with his friend Richard Lawrence. Grantham returned for another shipment of tobacco in the winter of 1675–1676, and when he left in March controversy was already building over the governor's handling of the Susquehannock War. When he next sailed to Virginia, in the autumn, it was at the helm of the *Concord*, which could carry 500 tons, fifty men, and thirty-two guns. The ship was among the largest and most heavily armed merchant vessels around.

Grantham sailed directly to the York River after entering the Chesapeake Bay, unaware that he was skirting Morris's dragnet at the mouth of the James River and just missing Berkeley as he returned to Accomack after the disastrous raid on the garrison at Councilor Bacon's house. The *Concord* rode up the wide lower reaches of the York on November 21, where Grantham discovered that the countryside was in rebellion. He immediately sent a boat across the Bay to Accomack. The *Concord*, he pledged, was at the governor's service. Delighted to have so much firepower at his disposal, Berkeley immediately joined Grantham.

Grantham, however, preferred diplomacy to war. That his ship's name was the *Concord*, he thought, was a sign from God. He was determined to promote "Tranquility and Good Understanding betwixt the Governor and the Rebels." Provided, that is, that the Governor prevailed: when Lawrence attempted to justify the rebellion to Grantham the captain replied that "nothing but a speedy Repentance could free him, and his Friends, and the Country from inevitable Ruin," signing his letter "Your very Loving Friend, (as far as my Allegiance to my King, and my Duty to my Governor will permit)."

With Berkeley's permission Grantham went "up into the Countrey to the Rebells," putting ashore on the north bank of the York and marching into the heart of Gloucester County. There he met with 800 men under Ingram at Pate's house. Shuttling back and forth between Pate's house and Berkeley's ship, Grantham convinced both Berkeley and the rebels to accept a cease-fire until the king's troops arrived by exploiting each side's confidence that the king would agree with its position once he had all the facts. In a show of force Ingram marched his men down the north shore of the York to Tindall's Point, where Berkeley could see them from the deck of his ship. While Grantham remained ashore as a hostage, Walklate was rowed out to formalize the truce.[12]

Christmas morning dawned "very fair." Aboard his ship on the York River, Berkeley was painfully aware that he had not yet established a foothold on land, nor even a perfect blockade of Virginia's many rivers. Some rebels were even managing to ship their tobacco aboard merchant vessels, "whereby," the governor protested, "the Rebels are encourag'd, and enabl'd to persist and continue in Rebellion." While rebels acquired "Goods and Necessaries" through this illegal trade, "those truly Loyal are forc'd from their Houses and Plantations, and their Estates seized, robb'd, and taken away." This unhappy situation would continue as long as the cease-fire was in effect.[13]

Berkeley might not have been so gloomy had he known what was happening a few miles away on the James. Early Christmas morning, thirty-plus men under Captain John Consett landed near William Groves's garrison on the south side of the James. The rebels, who had been taunting Consett's crew from ashore just the night before, were taken completely by surprise. They fled, leaving drums, banners, and ammunition strewn behind. The loyalists pursued Groves all day, finally overtaking his men and capturing several prisoners. Consett himself killed Groves. After spending the night aboard ship the loyalist party surprised the rebels who had returned to the garrison by attacking again the next morning, netting another thirteen prisoners and a boatload of plunder. The remnants of Groves's men fled to Arthur Allen's plantation, but they found no refuge there. Its commander Major Rookins and his men decamped on December 28, pausing only long enough to stuff linens, books, and other loot into pockets or pillowcases on their way out.

The loyalists had finally gained a foothold along the James. They now marched freely along the river's south shore without having to retreat to their ships at night.[14]

Along the York River the cease-fire signed by Walklate and Berkeley before Christmas lasted just three days.

Grantham blamed the rebels for breaking it, but still insisted on a diplomatic solution. Back he went to Pate's, passing to and fro several times during late December. He focused his attention on Ingram, who seemed to be looking for a way to "dismount from the back of that Horss," the rebellion. On January 1, 1677, Walklate secretly accepted a commission from Berkeley to command loyalist

The home of Berkeley loyalist Arthur Allen, now known as "Bacon's Castle," was a rebel garrison. Rebels looted the property during their stay, but it remains standing today. (Courtesy of Preservation Virginia)

troops, and the following day Ingram, Walklate, and 300 men under their command formally surrendered the vitally important West Point garrison. Grantham disabled their guns and sent the men to stay at Ingram's house. He would return, he told them, to formalize their surrender. Meanwhile they could count on unconditional pardons and console themselves with a cask of brandy.

From Ingram's house Grantham rode directly to another garrison at the home of Colonel John West. There he found the radical core of the rebellion: 400 "English and Negroes in Armes," including 250 servants and slaves who had been promised their freedom by Bacon. As Grantham later told the story, "some were for shooting mee, and others for cutting me in peeces." Grantham suggested a third option: he promised them their freedom and offered himself as a hostage until Berkeley confirmed it. Several hundred men surrendered and returned to their homes, but eighty slaves and twenty servants held out, hoping to join the Brick House garrison three miles away. Rather than fight such a desperate and well-armed group, Grantham agreed to let them take a small sloop from the garrison. Once aboard, the rebels discovered that Grantham had secretly removed its sails. They had little choice but to accept his offer to tow them to the Brick House.

As they approached the Brick House garrison the rebels spotted a fourteen-gun ship lying at anchor. To their horror, Grantham towed the rebel's sloop before the larger vessel and trained its guns on the rebels. If they did not give up their weapons, he threatened, he "would sinke and destroy them all." They surrendered "with a great deale of discontent, saying, had they knowne my resolution, they would have destroyed mee."

Disarmed, the holdouts were imprisoned on the *Concord* until Grantham could return them to their masters.

First, however, Grantham had to return to the rebels who had already surrendered. Sailing back upriver, he ordered the surrendered West Point garrison to march along the north shore of the York to Tindall's Point. In a contrast that could not have been lost on his cargo of slaves and servants, Grantham waited until they reached Tindall's Point to collect the other rebels' weapons, then administered an oath of obedience. After leading them in toasts to Charles II and Governor Berkeley, Grantham sent them home, as free as if there had never been a rebellion.

Some of the remaining rebel garrisons disbanded upon hearing of these reversals, but Drummond and Lawrence held out at the Brick House. Considered "the cheife Incendiarys, and promoters to and for Bacons Designes," they could expect to hang if captured. Reinforced by men fleeing from other garrisons, they gathered for a last-ditch effort to march upriver toward the frontier, hoping to pick up supporters along the way for a resurgent rebellion. Instead their force disintegrated, with men slipping off in ones and twos to make their way homeward or to start new lives outside of Virginia.

Away from the York River the fighting continued well into January. The last of the Rappahannock River rebels surrendered to Beverley on January 18, two weeks after Ingram and Walklate's capitulation. Along the James several hundred rebels laid siege to a loyalist fort, and only the threat of approaching enemy ships and mounted loyalists dislodged them. A week later Admiral Morris was still on his guard, having been warned that a rebel army "intends to surprise our fort." The loyalists rode out to meet the attackers, and in a midday battle they defeated the rebels and captured their commander. The following day the loyalist militia set off down the south side of the James "to settle that country." By January 19, Morris was able to deliver to the governor the "principal Rebells" taken in this final campaign.[15]

William Byrd might have hanged had he not been so nimble. He had recruited Bacon to lead the uprising and had remained with the rebels into the fall months. During the September raid on Augustine Warner's plantation, one of Bacon's soldiers later testified, "Capt. Bird was noe prisoner, but was in Arms, and reputed and held among the soldiers to be a Committee man, whose office was to dispose with goods as were ordered to be seized by Mr. Bacon." Yet somehow he was lucky enough, or clever enough, to maintain a relatively low profile throughout the struggle, so much so that loyalists seldom mentioned him in connection with the uprising.[16]

Then, on January 14, Byrd delivered into Admiral Morris's hands the former North Carolina governor William Drummond, who had been found half-starved in a swamp just above Jamestown. Still dressed in a gentleman's fur coat, Drummond was swiftly carried in irons to Governor Berkeley's ship on the York River. Several days later the two governors traveled together to Middle Plantation. Within a half-hour of their arrival Drummond had been tried and sentenced to death, and four hours later he was hanged alongside another less notorious rebel. Berkeley left the scene immediately, and on January 22 he was back home at Green Spring awaiting the seizure of other leading rebels. Byrd, however, was now safe from prosecution.[17]

Richard Lawrence simply disappeared. Thirty years later Thomas Mathew still wasn't sure what had become of him. "The last Account of Mr. Lawrence," he recalled, "was from an upper-most plantation, whence he and Four others Desperado's with horses pistolls etc. March'd away in a Snow Ancle Deep, who were thought to have Cast themselves into a Branch of some River, rather than to be treated like Drummond." But that was just a story, for which Mathew had no evidence except for Lawrence's disappearance. In the winter of 1677 there were still plenty of alternative stories in the air, offering very different accounts of his whereabouts and his plans.

Other fugitives did turn up, and Berkeley made sure their executions impressed upon as many Virginians as possible the price of treason. Some rebels had already been hanged on the Eastern Shore and at Middle Plantation. Now James Crews and several others were hanged at the trenches from which the rebels had besieged Jamestown. Others were hanged at gallows erected in the rebellious Southside counties. Four more were executed at Colonel Reade's on the York River, the garrison where Hansford had been captured in November. Still another rebel was suspended in chains on the gallows at West Point, left to die of thirst, starvation, and exposure, then to decay in public view, his rotting corpse and bleaching bones a monument to the fruits of treason.[18]

· *Seven* ·

# "A Seasonable Submission"

Berkeley had been home at Green Spring for only a week, mourning over the extensive damage done by the rebel garrison, when an urgent message arrived. The *Bristol* had entered the Chesapeake Bay carrying Sir John Berry, his fellow commissioner Francis Moryson, and seventy soldiers. Another thousand men under commissioner Herbert Jeffreys would arrive shortly. The elderly governor, who had been flattened by a fever a few days earlier, dragged himself from his sickbed, boarded an awaiting barge, sailed to the mouth of the James, and climbed unsteadily onto the *Bristol*'s rain-slick deck at noon on January 31, 1677, just two days after the ship's arrival.

The commissioners' instructions were to suppress the rebellion, to "enquire into and Report unto us, All such grievances and Pressures, which any of our Loving subjects . . . have suffer'd," and to make peace with the Indians. Their first reaction upon learning the state of affairs in Virginia was surprise: their instructions did not anticipate a scenario in which Berkeley was alive, Bacon was dead, and the rebellion was over. Even their most up-to-date information, acquired from a passing ship just a few days before their arrival, was four months out of date: it covered the burning of Jamestown, Bacon's "whole conquest of the Country," and his "givinge liberty to all Servants that followed him." Berry and Moryson were startled and impressed that the governor had matters so well in hand.

The next three days were "very gusty and stormy rainy weather," perfect for staying in one's cabin and "writinge [a] letter for England by a little Ketch," the *Henry & Jane*, that was about to sail for London. Berkeley, the commissioners gushed, had once again demonstrated his loyalty and worth to the crown. Just as no man had suffered more damage to his estate, "soe hath there been noe one (under God) a more eminent or active Instrument in suppressing this Rebellion." Berkeley had even anticipated the king's instructions by laying "a good foundation . . . of a Peace with the neighbor Indians" and scheduling a new Assembly for February 20. That left as the commissioners' only major task the collection of grievances to report to the king. Even that struck them as a simple task, for except for widespread complaints about the legislature's excessive salaries none had yet presented themselves. They expected to leave by June.

Yet Berkeley came away from the meeting sensing that something was wrong. Reading the papers from England after supper only added to his disquiet. He could see right away that there was plenty of room for disagreement over how to implement the king's instructions. Important documents conflicted with one another. One, dated October 1676, authorized Berkeley to decide whom to pardon, but another document, a printed proclamation from Charles II also dated October 1676, offered a pardon to all rebels who submitted within twenty days of its publication. Or did it? The language was unclear: it included the qualification "as the said Governor . . . shall approve of." Did this empower Berkeley to withhold pardons from some people, or did it refer only to the amount of the bond for good behavior that was to be required of former rebels? Still another document specified the wording of indictments for rebellion, implying that it was up to the government to decide who would stand trial and who would not.[1]

Clearly, how one implemented the king's instructions would depend upon how one understood the history and the present state of the rebellion. Berkeley concluded that he needed to tell the story of the rebellion in his own way. Indeed, he had already taken the precaution of preparing a report on an early September conversation between Bacon and one of his soldiers. Deceptively presented as if it were an actual transcript, the dialogue was actually a summary, months after the fact, dictated by Bacon's Henrico neighbor and follower John Goode. Goode was seeking a pardon from Berkeley for his role in the rebellion, and the "Discourse" was obtained through William Byrd. Eager to please Berkeley, Goode and Byrd produced just the document he needed.

The "Discourse" opened with a debate over whether the rebels could defeat a British army on Virginia soil (Bacon thought that they could, while Goode didn't) and then moved to the main point of the dialogue:

"Sir," Goode exclaimed, "you speak as though you designed a totall defection from Majestie and our native Country."

"Why," Bacon smiled, "have not many princes lost their dominions soe?"

"They have then beene such people as have beene able to subsist without their prince," protested Goode. How, he wondered, could Virginia survive without English imports, and without an English market for their tobacco? And what about attachments to "Parents, Friends and Correspondents in England?"

"I believe the King of France, or the States of Holland would either of them entertaine a trade with us."

"The followers doe not think themselves ingaged against the Kings Authority, but against the Indians," objected Goode. Besides, the French or Dutch had far more to lose by a war with England "then by any advantage they can reap by Virginia."

But Virginia was not alone, replied Bacon. Maryland and Carolina would also soon "cast of[f] their Governours," and even if that failed the rebels could easily take refuge in some remote district of North Carolina.

"Sir," objected Goode, "what you have discoursed will unavoidabely produce utter ruine, and destruction, to the people and Country, and I dread the thoughts of putting my hand to the promoteing a designe of such miserable Consequence."

"What should a Gentleman engaged as I am doe, you doe as good as tell me I must fly, or hang for it"?

"A Seasonable Submission" to the king's governor would suffice, suggested Goode. He left Bacon's army several days later and, in late January, ended this tale with his own seasonable appeal for mercy.[2]

Goode's "discourse" encapsulated the story that Berkeley wished to tell: one in which Bacon's designs were utterly subversive; his wickedness was apparent enough that his followers, like Goode, could choose freely to desert; and therefore in which Bacon's most active supporters were as unredeemable as the rebel himself.

Berkeley also took the precaution of dashing off his own account of the rebellion. Despite his fever, the old governor stayed up late in his cabin aboard ship preparing for Secretary of State Henry Coventry "a History of our miseries." He wrote in a rush, narrating events from memory. The resulting story wandered at some points, for which he apologized. At other points he skipped over weeks and months, omitting major characters and events. Running out of time, he reduced everything after the seige of Jamestown to a single paragraph, apologizing that "I must Epitomise the rest."

The point of the story, however, was clear. Featuring just a few episodes, the governor sketched out twin portraits of the rebel (prone to dishonor, deceit, cowardice, and self-advancement) and the governor (honorable, truthful, brave, and self-sacrificing). In these vignettes Bacon won supporters with lies and false promises. He resorted to an unmanly sneak attack against Virginia's Occaneechee allies. He even threatened to kill those foes who were wounded and had surrendered. In the end, it was irreligion that killed Bacon: in three deft sentences that effectively brought his story to a close, Berkeley related that Bacon had burned Jamestown's church with his "owne sacreligious hands," but that God swiftly "Overtooke him." Since Bacon's favorite oath was "God damme my Blood," God had granted his wish: he "so infected his blood that it bred lice in incredible number so that for twenty dayes he never washt his shirts but burned them."

Berkeley dated his "History" February 2, 1677, the day after his initial meeting with Berry and Moryson. He sent it to Secretary of State Coventry via the *Henry & Jane* that same day. The ketch lingered a few more days before sailing to England with both Berkeley's and the commissioners' correspondence aboard.[3]

Not content to leave it at that, Berkeley also engaged the new Assembly he had called to meet at Green Spring on February 20 to support his cause. Ignoring a request from the commissioners demanding action on points of their choosing, the Burgesses roundly applauded Berkeley's performance, begged Charles II to retain him as governor, and provided a loyalist account of the rebellion. They withheld pardons from fifty-five "notorious actors" and ordered that the estates of convicted rebels be forfeited to the crown. As commanded by Charles II, the Burgesses voided all of the laws from the June Assembly and then reenacted those that had not been extorted by Bacon.[4]

Berkeley and the commissioners agreed that the conflict was not yet spent. From the moment they arrived Jeffreys, Moryson, and Berry fretted about the whereabouts of Lawrence, "a most stubborne resolved and desperate Rebell . . . fitt to head a new faction," and they took the precaution of dispatching British regulars to garrison rebel strongholds. Berkeley, the Assembly, and the commissioners all worked, as well, to confirm the legitimacy of the Indian slave trade while also imposing tough new treaties on the Pamunkeys and other "tributary" nations that would bring peace, but also blunt criticisms that they were favoring Indians over colonists.

Under these circumstances the Pamunkey werowansqua Cockacoeske quickly accepted an invitation to meet with the Royal Commissioners to negotiate a new treaty, gathering in May 1677 along with the representatives of several other nearby nations at the main British garrison of Middle Plantation. In a matter of days the Indians had agreed to accept Charles II as their sovereign and to fight alongside Virginians against "forreigne" Indians. In return the commissioners, confessing that the conflict had begun with their own people's "violent Intrusions" onto Indian lands, confirmed Native possession of those lands and their fishing, gathering, and hunting rights throughout Virginia. Not least, the Indian parties to the treaty also gained new protections against enslavement by Virginians. Enemy Indians, however, could still be sold as slaves.

While not generous, the treaty was far better than what Bacon's followers had in mind. On the king's birthday, May 29, it was read aloud and translated paragraph-by-paragraph. Cockacoeske and the werowances of the Weyanoks, Nansemonds, and Nottaways signed one copy and delivered it to Jeffreys "upon their Knees." Still kneeling, they accepted the copy that Jeffreys had signed and passed it from hand to hand, each "kissing the Paper . . . until every one had done the like Mark of Reverence to it." Berry and Moryson considered it a "sign of a most free and joyfull acceptance of this Peace."[5]

Berkeley, however, did not attend the Treaty of Middle Plantation. He was well out to sea, several weeks into an unhappy voyage to England. He was bound for London, having been recalled as governor by a wrathful Charles II. Berkeley arrived in June 1677 and settled in while waiting to see the king. Once again he took up the pen, this time appealing directly to Charles II. He reminded his majesty that he had fought for his father Charles I during the Civil Wars, and that in thirty-five years as governor he had taken

Cockacoeske was given this frontlet as a memento of the 1677 Treaty of Middle Plantation. (Courtesy of Preservation Virginia; photograph by Katherine Wetzel)

Virginia from near-ruin to a flourishing colony that contributed £100,000 per year in customs revenues. He had "lived in much love and care with the Inhabitants" until Bacon came along, and in quelling the rebellion he had hazarded his life and suffered financial ruin. What was truly unbearable, however, was that his actions had been blatantly misrepresented to the king, causing him to be recalled to England in disgrace. His long service, the rough passage to England, and grief over his mistreatment had ruined his health. His humble prayer to the king, the seventy-two-year-old governor concluded, was "to cleare his Innocency before he dyes."

Why did Berkeley feel disgraced? Clearly someone had told a more compelling story than he had. It may have made a difference that the homes of the colony's leading loyalists had been trashed, forcing Berkeley to billet the commissioners with councilor Thomas Swann, whose home had been spared by rebel looters because he had signed Bacon's Oath. Somewhere, perhaps at Swann's dinner table, the commissioners heard, accepted, and then told in great detail to imperial authorities, a narrative of the rebellion in which *Berkeley* was the villain.[6]

By March 1677 the commissioners had come to the conclusion that "those who stile themselves the Loyall Party" were the "chiefe Disturbers and Obstructers of the Peace." The trouble, they decided, had started between the end of the rebellion and the commissioners' arrival. Berkeley and his men had tried and punished rebels using military justice even though their prisoners had been captured after the rebellion, in time of peace. They had also hanged men who fell under the king's pardon and had looted the estates of rebels with no pretense of due process.

Troubles multiplied after the arrival of Berry and Moryson, this version asserted. Berkeley resisted publishing the king's October 1676 notice pardoning all rebels who submitted within twenty days. When he did reluctantly issue it on February 11 he supplemented it with his own proclamation withholding pardon from numerous leading rebels, contrary to both the king's will and to justice: many rebels, after all, had been seduced or intimidated into joining Bacon.[7]

Worse, when Colonel Jeffreys arrived at Green Spring he had delivered the king's direct order for Berkeley to return to England, leaving Jeffreys to govern in his absence. Rather than comply, Berkeley obtained an opinion from his Council that he could return to England whenever it was expedient. In the meantime, the commissioners charged, Berkeley enriched himself and his friends. He allowed loyalists to raid their enemies' plantations with impunity. He manipulated the trials of accused rebels with the same results, pardoning some men for their lives while confiscating their estates for treason, then seizing their goods for his own use. When the commissioners asked for an accounting of the confiscated goods Berkeley simply ignored them.

Had not the king's pardon arrived in time to restrain Berkeley, the commissioners' story went, there would have been "a new Disturbance kindled and broke out, great as the former." So many people had joined the rebellion that without a general pardon there could be no lasting peace. Besides, many of Bacon's followers had been forced to act "against their Allegiance and conscience." Berkeley's vindictive persecutions posed a greater danger to the peace than such half-hearted rebels.[8]

Furthermore, Berkeley had gone out of his way to insult the king's commissioners. He demanded to inspect their instructions, as if to insinuate that they were making them up as they went along. And in mid-April, when he booked passage for England, he made it known that he meant to take his case directly to England rather than trusting the commissioners to report fairly on the rebellion. The final insult, reported the commissioners, had come on April 22 when they visited Green Spring to say farewell to the governor. When Berkeley's coach drew up to carry the commissioners home they recognized the driver as the colony's executioner. This was simply too much. Rather than accept the ride, they stalked down the road to the landing several miles away. Nursing their anger as they returned to their lodgings at Swann's, they "resolved to make his Majestie himselfe a Judge in this High

Indignitie offered to us." In one last unkind cut, when Berkeley departed several days later he predicted to Jeffreys that "the inhabitants of this Colony will quickly find a difference between your management and mine."[9]

Berkeley and his supporters wove the same events into a completely different story. Crucially, in the loyalists' version of the rebellion very few men had been seduced or frightened into treason; rather, Bacon's followers chose their course of action—freely, deliberately, and repeatedly. The war also lasted longer in Berkeley's narrative than it did in the commissioners': the peacetime impressments of food and horses that the commissioners objected to actually happened in wartime, as they were mistaken about the date of the rebellion's conclusion. (They thought it had ended with the surrender of West Point on January 2, so that confiscations during the continued fighting after that date did not register, for them, as wartime actions.) Berkeley also flatly denied converting confiscated goods to his own use; rather, those goods supplied the loyalist forces that had defeated the rebels and restored the king's peace. In objecting to such seizures the commissioners wrongly admonished him "for that which was ever practis'd in al nations," including England. While fighting alongside the king's father against Parliament in the 1640s, for example, Berkeley had personally heard Charles I "Order to cease [seize] the houses, goods and cattle of many that had declared against him." By pressing the point, the commissioners were punishing loyalism while rewarding treason: rebels' complaints of looting were heard sympathetically, Berkeley complained, but "no hopes given to the Loyal party to recover the least part of their losses."[10]

Berkeley's version of events differed even more radically in describing events after the rebellion. According to him, the printed proclamation of October 1676 was neither completely applicable to the situation in Virginia nor entirely consistent with the king's other instructions. Charles had directed Berkeley to call a new Assembly, convene special courts, and negotiate an Indian treaty, which obviously meant that he was to remain until he had fulfilled his instructions. Certainly the king had not meant for Jeffreys to assume power before Berkeley had left Virginia. And as for the accusation that he had assigned the hangman to drive the commissioners' coach, "I never saw the fellows face but once before, and did not know that he was in my house."

Berkeley waited in London for weeks without gaining an audience with Charles II. On June 16 he finally received word from Secretary of State Coventry that "his Majesty would like to speak with you," but by then Berkeley was so ill, "so unlike to live," Coventry said, that "it had been inhuman to have troubled him." William Berkeley died on July 9, 1677, Coventry reported, "without any accompt given of his Government." The governor's body, encased in lead foil, was laid to rest four days later in the vault of a parish church near his brother's country home. Frances, still at Green Spring, wrote a final letter to her husband on August 9, as yet unaware of his death.[11]

Had he lived to see the king Berkeley would have been disappointed. Reports and documents from the commissioners arrived in England in late April and early May. Rather than letting Charles read the documents for himself, Secretary Coventry summarized them into a list whose wording effectively resolved most issues in the commissioners' favor. Thus Charles had already made up his mind while Berkeley was en route to England. "Wee are not a little surprised," he wrote on May 13, "that you make difficulty to yeild obedience" to the command to return to England, it "being so clear and plaine that Wee thought no man could have raised any doubt or dispute concerning the same." Coventry elaborated for the king, calling Berkeley's failure to return one of two great errors (along with altering the king's October 1676 proclamation by exempting people from the king's pardon). "His Majesty is very sensible of these miscarriages, and hath very little hope that the people of Virginia shall be brought to a right sense of their duty to their Governors when the Governors themselves will not obey the King."[12]

Moryson and Berry returned to England at the end of the summer and submitted a final report that included a "Narrative of the Rise, Progresse and Cessation of the Late Rebellion." The "Narrative" detailed events prior to Bacon's death at great length, but compressed Bacon's final illness and the months of bitter fighting that followed into just two brief paragraphs. The effect was to support the notion that the rebels had been seduced or intimidated by Bacon rather than willingly and repeatedly choosing rebellion even after his death. Another theme in the commissioners' report was that credit for the victory over the rebels belonged to the ships' captains, not to "those that assume to themselves the name of the Loyall Party and brag soe highly of their great deeds and mighty manhood." By downplaying the rebels' tenacity after Bacon's death and the role of land forces under Beverley and other loyalist commanders, the commissioners eliminated elements of the story that conflicted with their portrayal of the loyalists as the true disturbers of the king's peace. Most significantly—though this would have pleased Berkeley—the commissioners' report left out the multitude of complaints they had received in response to their call for grievances from the counties, many of which called for the same reforms the Baconites had demanded before and during the rebellion.[13]

Berkeley's death put an end to his problems, but not to Virginia's or the crown's—let alone to those of the Indians. The rebellion had been fought over far more serious matters than a mere personal struggle between the Berkeley and Bacon. Fundamental issues remained unresolved, and the people with the most at stake in the conflict still did not know their fates. What would become of the Susquehannocks, Occaneechees, Pamunkeys, and Piscataways? How would the Indians, from the Five Nations in the North to the Westos and other Carolina nations in the South, withstand the combined onslaught of land-hungry planters, English slavers, and genocidal militias? The war had started with Indians, and no one had more at stake in these events than Indians. There could be no real resolution to the conflict that did not resolve the Indians' problems—or the colonists' problems with Indians.

The ordinary planters who had supported Bacon in such large numbers had serious difficulties of their own, which also had yet to be resolved. Despite having managed to keep their lives and property after their unsuccessful rebellion, they were no closer to finding their way out from under the weight of heavy taxation, political powerlessness, labor shortages, and other economic problems. They still believed that Indians were being coddled and allowed to threaten the colony, and their hunger for Indian land and slaves was far from satisfied. For these planters gaining control of Indian land and labor remained the key to establishing personal independence, attracting a wife, supporting a family, and otherwise achieving full manhood. Servants and slaves, of course, labored under an even greater weight, perhaps all the more so after the failed promise of freedom that had drawn many of them into Bacon's army.

The system worked much better for elite planters such as Byrd and Beverley, but its dangerous instability had them worried too. Could they maintain their privileged position? Factions among the elite had made it impossible for many of them to fight on the same side during the rebellion, and unless they could present a more united front in the future they would remain vulnerable to another, perhaps more radical, rebellion. Charles II, Lord Baltimore, and their appointed officials faced the same specter of rebellion on a greater scale, with not only their income and their authority at stake, but also the well-being of the subjects for whom they were responsible. Could the provincial governments afford another war without pushing the colonies' heavily taxed planters into another insurrection? Or would those same people demand more Indian wars regardless of the expense, and rebel again if they thought that their governors were failing to protect them from the "savages"?

To compound these difficulties, yet another crisis was under way and headed for America. A fundamental reexamination of England's religious settlement, dynastic politics, foreign policy, and indeed its very identity was in progress, all occasioned by the twists and turns of the king's family life. Combining sex, politics, and religion, a series of bitter controversies over Charles II and his brother James threatened to encompass the colonies' existing crises and raise the stakes involved in the resolution of Bacon's Rebellion to a seemingly cosmic level. Bacon's Rebellion, it was evident, had been but Part One of an unfolding tragedy.

*Part Two*

# "THE SECOND PART OF THE LATE TRAGEDY"

## · Eight ·

# STRANGE INDIANS AND POPISH PLOTS

Bacon's followers laid down their arms but did not abandon the struggle. Late in 1676, while the royal commissioners were still under sail from England and loyalist forces were just beginning to score major victories over the rebels, an anonymous colonist penned a "Complaint from Heaven with a Huy and crye and a petition out of Virginia and Maryland." Addressing himself to the king, Parliament, and the lord mayor and alderman of London, the author wrote that Bacon's death merely marked the end of the first act of the play. "Now," the author warned, "begins the second part of the late tragedy." He predicted a "longe destructive warr" in which everything that truly mattered was at stake. Nothing less than the grand struggle between God and Satan was being played out in America, through the actions of their Protestant, Catholic, and Indian surrogates.

"It is high time, that the originall Cause" of Bacon's Rebellion was revealed, the "Complaint" began. The "Barklian and Baltimorian Parties" had disguised their real intentions, which were "to overturn England with feyer, sword, and distractions [and] drive us

Protestants to Purgatory within our selves in America, with the help of the French spirits from Canada." Berkeley himself might not be fully aware of this grand plot, the writer speculated, because profits from the Indian trade had blinded him to the Indians' treachery. This, in fact, was part of the Catholic Lord Baltimore's plan, for "it is his Custome to exchaince the King's Majesty's Subjects, for furr."

Baltimore posed an even greater danger to the people than Berkeley did. He had made a show of sending troops against the Susquehannocks in 1675 but had actually hindered the Virginians. Tricking the Virginians into besieging their fort when an immediate assault would have carried the day, Baltimore bought the Susquehannocks precious time to gain strength. After breaking the siege, the Susquehannocks had killed at least 500 colonists without meeting any resistance until "Squire Bacon, moved with the peoples and his owne loss," had momentarily "repulsed" them.

Having unleashed the Indians upon the frontiers, Baltimore next set out to cover up his crimes. He tried to silence Major Truman, commander of the Maryland troops, by prosecuting him for killing the Susquehannock emissaries while under a white flag. Why, the author of the "Complaint from Heaven" wanted to know, was Truman blamed for this, since the Susquehannocks were known murderers? Clearly Baltimore intended to "stop his [Truman's] mouth and prevent his complaininge to England, to reveal secrets."

To add insult to injury, Baltimore used the very Indian wars that he had fomented as pretexts to oppress the people. He "tooke all the plunder from the poor Souldiers," sold the Indians they had captured into slavery in Barbados, kept the profits, and forced the colonists to pay high wartime taxes. Yet despite these taxes there never seemed to be enough weapons in the armories. That too, of course, was part of the plan "to yoak the inhabitants" while enriching himself in the process.

Why, though, would Baltimore embrace the Indians and oppress his own countrymen? The answer was obvious: he was a Catholic first, and an Englishman in name only. Look who ruled Maryland: the government was packed with Calvert family members and other "strong Papists" while an even more powerful shadow government, a "secret Councell of priests and Natives," operated behind the scenes. Behind them stood the pope, and behind him, Satan. The key to the plot was a small group of French Jesuit missionaries from Canada, "Pope's messengers" who lived among the Iroquois, "connivinge with Maryland papists" and the Indians to destroy the Protestants.

Who, then, were the real traitors in Bacon's Rebellion? "Are wee Rebells because wee will not submit to their arbitrary government and intangle our innocent posterity under that tyranicall yoake of papacy?" Bacon's Rebellion was properly understood as a valiant attempt at foiling a wicked plot to bring the Protestants "into a confusion and ruynated nothing." In the petitioners' opinion the plot was working all too well, for with Berkeley beginning to punish some of the more prominent Baconites, the papist-Indian alliance had successfully "prevayled with the Virginians to hange their best comon wealths men out of the way." The "Complaint from Heaven" made it clear that Bacon's followers regarded their military defeat at Berkeley's hands as a temporary setback—not as the end of the affair, but as the occasion for a shift in strategy.[1]

Maryland's Governor Thomas Notley utterly rejected the "Complaint's" cosmic view of events, but he certainly agreed that Bacon's

Rebellion was not yet over. The very existence of the "Complaint" demonstrated that. Maryland's Baconites, Notley warned, would have long since joined the rebellion had they not lacked a local leader. But one might still be found, for "the warme weather when it comes may produce another swarme, that may have as venomous stings, as the late traytor had."

To avoid this shipwreck, Notley needed to end the expensive and destabilizing Susquehannock War. In an April 1677 Council meeting in St. Mary's City it was decided to send Henry Coursey, a wealthy Irish-born Eastern Shore planter with minimal experience in Indian diplomacy, to make peace with the northern Indians. Coursey's first stop was New York, where he would consult with Governor Andros. He reached the town on June 6, ferrying across the wide Hudson toward the imposing stone walls of Ft. James. Governor Andros awaited him. Coursey's diplomatic education was about to begin in earnest.

Andros immediately recognized that the proposal Coursey intended to deliver to the Five Nations was unacceptable. During the spring their warriors had rounded up many of the Susquehannocks living along the Susquehanna and Delaware rivers and forcibly resettled them in Iroquois towns. Yet Coursey intended to claim that Maryland had conquered the Susquehannocks and to demand that the Iroquois accept Maryland's jurisdiction over them. The Five Nations would never do so. Moreover, there was too much talk of victory and conquest, and too little of peace and harmony, to suit Iroquois sensibilities. Nor could Andros himself agree to Coursey's plan, for there was no role for New York in the proposed arrangements.

It took Andros several weeks to bring Coursey around, tutoring him in the basics of Iroquois treaty protocol and rewriting Maryland's opening proposal to make it more acceptable to New York and the Iroquois. The new version omitted all mention of the Susquehannocks, silently conceding that they would live within and be subordinate to the Five Nations. Rather than making a separate peace between the Iroquois and the Chesapeake colonies, it included New York and recognized Andros as the king's representative to the Five Nations. The Iroquois and their dependent nations would trade with New York, but not with the southern colonies.

Finally satisfied, Andros convened the treaty in Albany in August 1677. The negotiations took several weeks, far longer than the inexperienced Marylanders had expected. Coursey learned a great deal about Indian diplomacy in the process, and thanks to Andros he returned to Maryland with an important and enduring treaty. However, he failed to register the single most important feature of the peace agreement he had signed. In the Five Nations' opening speech the Onondaga orator Garacontié spoke of a "Covenant Chain," forged of silver, that would henceforth bind the Five Nations to New York and extend, through the addition of more links, to other English colonies and Indian nations. Andros, who saw more clearly than Coursey that the treaty increased New York's power by putting it at the center of the Covenant Chain, gladly embraced the new diplomatic system it promised to create.[2]

It soon became apparent that Coursey's treaty had failed to put a stop to Susquehannock and Iroquois raids against Virginia, Maryland, and their neighbor Indians. Within two years of Coursey's treaty the conflicts were already starting to escalate, because the basic cultural imperatives that inspired Iroquois men to go to war continued unabated. Each spring young men, directed by leading women to find captives to replace loved ones who had died (and eager to prove themselves as warriors), set out toward distant nations who were not part of the Covenant Chain. For some of these warriors the route to the towns of the Occaneechees and other southern peoples passed through frontier settlements in Virginia. Inevitably they ran into "some indiscreet or rather Mad men" among the Virginians who violated the peace agreement. The bloodiest fighting took place at Henrico, where five English were killed and six captured. Two northern warriors died in the fighting, and somehow an Iroquois woman, the granddaughter of a powerful sachem named Swerisse, fell into English hands. Swerisse's granddaughter became a slave, seemingly beyond rescue in the island colony of Bermuda.[3]

Part of the problem was that few Virginians or Marylanders understood that for Indians, alliances depended not upon written treaties but upon regular face-to-face meetings at which the terms of the peace were reaffirmed in speeches and confirmed by the giving and acceptance of gifts. The sense of reciprocity created by the exchange of gifts and hospitality, the familiarity bred over the weeks of negotiations, and the common interests created and continuously reaffirmed by regular trade relations were meant to create a fundamental sense of affection and goodwill that would, more than the details of the treaty, ensure peaceable relations.

A quixotic mission in the winter of 1678–1679 by one man, a Potomac River Native who had been taken away by the Iroquois as a youth, imparted some of these lessons to southern colonists. In the years since his capture, he said, he had "received soe much civility and kindness" from the Seneca Nation Iroquois who had adopted him that when he was away he missed them as much as he did the friends of his childhood. In December 1678, with Coursey's treaty in danger of falling apart, he took it upon himself to go home to the Potomac and explain "who it was had Done the English all the mischiefe": not the majority of the Iroquois people, but rather a small minority with an implacable hatred of the colonists and their neighbor Indians. Alone, he slogged through the snowy, mountainous terrain that lay between Iroquoia and the Chesapeake colonies, emerging from the woods and approaching the palisades of the Piscataway fort in early March. The Piscataway leaders whisked him to a meeting with Governor Calvert (freshly returned from England) at Mattapany, Calvert's fortified brick mansion outside St. Mary's City.

At Mattapany the Seneca was the center of attention. As the English and Piscataways watched he theatrically laid down five pine cones, spacing them in an arc across Calvert's table. These, he explained, were the five different nations of the Iroquois. Then he clustered three more cones around the first cone on the western end; these represented the four towns of the Seneca Nation. Around the next cone he laid another three, making a second cluster of four cones signifying the towns of the adjoining Cayuga nation. Among the Cayuga towns, he said, the "two middlemost" had taken in the Susquehannocks. There were other towns in other nations, he explained, and he could have laid down many more pine cones. But those towns were not the problem, because only the men from the Cayuga-Susquehannock towns had attacked the frontiers. Safe in their northern towns, "the Susquehannocks laugh and jeare at the English saying they cann doe what mischief they please for that the English cannot see them."

Who did the Susquehannocks intend to attack next, asked Calvert? The Piscataways' speaker answered for the Seneca, interjecting that another former captive who had recently escaped from the Iroquois had heard "the Greate man of the Susquehannocks" say that "he was pretty well Satisfied with the Revenge he had taken of the Virginians. . . . And now did intend to fall upon the Pascattoway Indians and the English in Maryland." A war party was already on its way.

There was little more to be said, but the Piscataways seized the moment by presenting the Seneca with a wampum belt. "The Axe seems to be laid at our heads for the present," their speaker said. "Yett wee intend to send this Belt as a token of our Love" to the Iroquois. The Seneca promised to deliver it "as a token of Friendshipp and Amity from the Emperour of Pascattoway." Calvert hastened to say that he would soon send presents as well. It was not a full-blown treaty, but it was a proper gesture and a promising sign of better diplomatic relations to come.[4]

Virginians, who had suffered more at the hands of northern raiders than Marylanders, were also beginning to see the need for more continuous and personal diplomacy with the Iroquois. Lieutenant Governor Chicheley, acting as governor until the recently deceased Herbert Jeffreys could be replaced, somehow managed to retrieve Swerisse's granddaughter from slavery in Bermuda. He dispatched an emissary, Colonel William Kendall, to Albany in late September 1679 to redeem her and to renew Coursey's treaty.

But Kendall demonstrated that Indian diplomacy was a lost art in Virginia. He neglected to conduct a standard opening ceremony at Albany and then delivered an inappropriately unfriendly opening speech. Although everyone was pleased with the return of Swerisse's granddaughter and the Iroquois' release of the six Virginians captured at Henrico in 1678, the negotiations continued in an unpleasant tone that was at odds with the studied politeness called for in Iroquois diplomacy. For weeks Kendall and a variety of Iroquois speakers traded accusations of breaches of the 1677 treaty and wrangled over the return of additional captives. Only with difficulty did the two sides agree to set aside their past grievances and to better observe the terms of the Coursey treaty.[5]

Despite this flurry of diplomatic activity, hundreds of Susquehannock and Iroquois warriors traveled south in the spring of 1680. They arrived along the Potomac in early May while Piscataway and Mattawoman women were still busy planting the summer's corn and the men were tending to their fish traps. Filtering down the familiar draws above Piscataway Creek on a Sunday morning, concealing their approach in the spring canopy of fresh-leaved trees, the northerners drew tantalizingly close before someone sounded the alarm at the last moment. Piscataway men slowed the attackers' approach just enough to allow the townspeople to flee to the fort and secure its gates. The northerners, however, could afford to be patient. It took only a part of their force to pin down the Piscataways while the rest fished, hunted, and feasted on Piscataway horses. There was nothing the Piscataways could do, the Susquehannocks taunted, to prevent them from revenging their "greate men killed in the late war."

When a small force of Maryland rangers appeared a few days later, though, the northerners drew back into the woods, maintaining a loose siege while avoiding direct conflict with the colonists. The siege was further weakened because the Susquehannocks lacked canoes to prevent the Piscataways from getting about by water. They were also reluctant to follow the Piscataways when they began building a new fort at Zachia Swamp, much closer to the English settlements. By late July the Piscataways had all moved to the new fort. The besiegers melted away, and as the threat receded the Piscataways moved back to their main town.

The Susquehannocks' setback, however, was only temporary. They returned for their revenge in February 1681, trekking southward through the snow and mud and crossing icy rivers in a rare midwinter attack against the Mattawomans, close neighbors and allies to the Piscataways and to Maryland. The surprise was complete. In the space of a few hours they had nearly destroyed the Mattawomans as a people and were already on their way back north with coffles of prisoners, among them the Mattawomans' hereditary chief—their werowance.

The catastrophe at Mattawoman "struck such dread and terror" into the other neighbor Indians that months later, when the time came to plant the summer's crops, they were still too fearful to go into the fields. The Piscataways retreated to their fort at Zachaia Swamp, where Maryland's government sent them arms and ammunition. Everyone, it seemed, believed that the Susquehannocks would return for the Piscataways.[6]

Affairs were no more settled on Virginia's southern flank, where William Byrd, Abraham Wood, and other frontier-dwellers still owed their livelihoods to commerce with the Indians. With the Occaneechees out of the way, the Virginians could trade more freely with other groups. But with whom? The Southern Piedmont was in considerable ferment, with the Occaneechees and other groups scattering to the south and west and bumping up against other nations that were also moving, shifting alliances, and combining into new, multiethnic towns and confederations.

These conflicts created new opportunities for Indian traders. Warring Indian nations took captives from one another, and Virginia's Assembly seized the opening. Building upon earlier laws permitting Virginians to keep Indians they took in war as slaves, the Burgesses ruled that captives taken by Virginia's Indian allies could be sold to colonists as slaves. With this legal sanction, a steadily increasing flow of Indian captives accompanied English traders back to the falls of the James to be absorbed into Virginians' households or sold to West Indian planters.[7]

The instability on Virginia's southern flank peaked between 1680 and 1682 with the collapse of the Westos, who had prospered since the 1660s by raiding throughout the southeast for Indian slaves to be sold to Virginia and Carolina traders. Not surprisingly, the Westos had made many enemies. Even their colonial trading partners could not be counted upon: Virginia traders increasingly preferred trading with the more populous Tuscaroras and Cherokees, who had better access to beaver pelts and deerskins, while Carolina's proprietors, concerned with military security, began to distance themselves from the much-hated Westos. By June 1680 Carolina had resolved to prohibit trading weapons and ammunition with the Westos and to negotiate a new, more restrictive treaty with them.

Worse for the Westos, the Carolina treaty negotiations turned out to be a trap. In the midst of the negotiations, their emissaries were seized, killed, and scalped by the English. Shocked, the Westos turned to their nearest allies, the Savannahs, to mediate a peace with Carolina. The Savannahs, however, took *these* Westo emissaries and sold them into slavery, launching a bitter war in which the Savannahs killed and enslaved so many Westos that they nearly ceased to exist. Hundreds were sold as slaves for the West Indian sugar plantations, others fled north to be absorbed into the Five Nations, and still others moved westward into a new village among predominantly Creek Indian towns. Virginia and Carolina traders moved on, finding other sources of Indian slaves: Tuscaroras and Yamasees in coastal Carolina or, farther west, Catawbas, Creeks, Cherokees, and Chickasaws. The changing sources of slaves, furs, and pelts did not matter so much to the English, so long as the supplies continued.[8]

The greatest source of instability, however, lay not in Indian country but in England. A steady flow of news from across the Atlantic had, in the 1670s, concerned the sex lives and religious practices of Charles II and his younger brother James, Duke of York. Charles's exploits were the subject of poems and satires circulating in manuscript form, but despite siring at least fourteen children by various mistresses he had no children by the queen. That left James as the heir to the throne, with his daughters Mary and Anne in line after him.

It also left the English public with a major political problem. Although Catholicism had been largely suppressed in England by

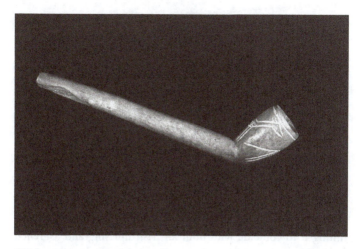

This ceramic pipe, dating to the 1670s, was found near Jamestown at the residence of an indentured servant or tenant farmer. Combining features typical of pipes made by English colonists, African Americans, and Native Americans, it nicely captures the close, complicated relations between these groups, as well as the centrality of tobacco and the importance of Indians in colonial Virginia. (Courtesy of Xanterra Corporation)

the end of the sixteenth century, there was a general perception that Catholics occupied too many high places in government. To weed them out Parliament passed the Test Act in 1673, requiring officeholders to take an oath that effectively forced them to choose between being Catholic and keeping their positions.

James refused to take the oath. Then, in case there was any remaining doubt that the heir to the throne was a Catholic, he married Mary of Modena, a devoutly Catholic princess from an Italian duchy closely allied with Louis XIV of France. Almost immediately there was talk of excluding James from the throne in favor of his Protestant daughter from his first marriage (also named Mary), or for limiting James's authority in religious affairs if he became king, or for requiring that his children by Mary of Modena be raised as Protestants. There was even a successful movement to arrange a marriage between James's daughter Mary and her cousin William of Orange, a fiercely Protestant Dutch military commander who was rapidly becoming the greatest obstacle to the growth of French power under Louis XIV.[9]

In the summer of 1678 the English public's attention was riveted by the unmasking of a "Popish Plot." Jesuit priests, it was said, had arranged for the assassination of Charles II, masterfully timing it to coincide with both an Irish uprising and a French invasion. Although skeptics pointed out that the creators of this story, Titus Oates and Isreal Tonge, were suspiciously vague about how this complicated series of events was supposed to have been arranged and were at a loss to explain certain contradictions in their testimony, the story was too interesting, and too well matched to English Protestants' fears and preconceptions about Catholics, to be dismissed. Any lingering doubts about Oates's reliability were dispelled when the justice of the peace who had taken Oates's initial deposition was found strangled and stabbed to death with his own sword. Panicked, the nation mobilized against the anticipated Catholic uprising and French and Spanish invasions. Dozens of alleged plotters were arrested.

At the height of this panic the House of Commons learned of a secret pact, made in 1668, in which France's Louis XIV had agreed to subsidize Charles II in return for Catholic-friendly government policies. Horrified members of Parliament leaped to pass a bill excluding Catholics from the throne, which everyone understood to be directed against James. Charles angrily dissolved Parliament rather than allow it to pass such an exclusion bill, but he could not suppress the growing belief among his subjects that "Popery and slavery, like two sisters, go hand in hand . . . wheresoever the one enters, the other is always following close at hand."[10]

News of the Popish Plot began trickling into Virginia and Maryland during the winter of 1678–1679. Among the most enthusiastic newshounds was Josias Fendall, the fervently Protestant former governor who had led the attempted coup against the Calverts' government in 1660. Maryland's Governor Notley had kept a close eye on him during Bacon's Rebellion; had he not, Lord Baltimore was convinced, Fendall would have "certainly joined with Bacon," and Maryland would have been "imbroiled and ruined as Virginia was." Indeed, Fendall was a likely suspect as the author of the "Complaint from Heaven." Now, with new revelations about the Popish Plot arriving by each ship, Fendall began collecting "the late proceedings in England" at his plantation on a small creek not far from Governor Notley's estate.

With England finally alert to the Catholic menace, Fendall hoped that the suffering of his fellow Protestants might soon end. "The time was comeing," he told anyone who would listen. When it did, he would have no trouble raising "Disaffected persons enough at the Cliffes" to secure the colony against Baltimore. All Fendall awaited was a signal to act.[11]

## · *Nine* ·

# "An Itching Desire"

THE WATERWAYS NEAR THOMAS MATHEW'S HOME WERE alive with dugout canoes in the spring of 1681 as Indians from as far away as the Rappahannock River and the Eastern Shore traded, tended to their spring fisheries, and found temporary work with English planters. One party of three women, three men, and two children worked at making dugout canoes for English planters that spring, living on each client's property for two or three weeks while the men toiled over a "great tree" they had felled, stripped of its branches, and hollowed out with slow fires.

The canoe-makers spent several weeks working for the powerful Nicholas Spencer, secretary of the Virginia Council and customs collector for the Potomac River. Spencer provided a small house for them to sleep in. The women gathered berries and cooked; occasionally the men hunted with guns borrowed from the English. A passing canoe of Indians coming from the Eastern Shore visited one day, but otherwise the canoe-makers had little contact with outsiders. Thus they had no way of realizing that a horrific murder had taken place at Point Lookout, just a few miles away near the mouth of the Potomac. Indians, it seemed, had killed four Englishmen and a woman at their own home.

Shortly after leaving Spencer's the canoe-makers crossed paths with a ship's crew searching for the killers. They were promptly arrested. At their trial in late June they were acquitted on the strength of Spencer's testimony that they had been working on his property when the murders were committed. Some English, however, insisted that they had been mixed up in the killings; witnesses at the trial testified that they had been caught with property stolen from the murder victims. Other neighbor Indians from the Rappahannock, Potomac, or Eastern Shore were also said to be involved.[1]

Josias Fendall had been expecting something like the murders at Point Lookout. Several weeks before the killings he had encountered John Dent on a country road.

"What news Mr. Dent"?

"I live in the Forrest where we have little or news stirring."

"What," asked Fendall, "do you hear no news of . . . the Papists joyning with the [Iroquois]. Do you not hear," he said, "what my Lord [Baltimore] has done?"

"No," replied Dent. "What is it?"

"He sent a party of men to apprehend me," Fendall lied. But if the Protestants could arrest Baltimore and a handful of his most important Catholic supporters, then "the rest of the Papists signified nothing."

"You should [wait for] a Comission out of England," said Dent.

"It would be too late."

Turning the conversation to the Indian situation, Dent asked Fendall "what do you think of it truly"?

"The Papists and Indians joyn together."

"Captain Fendall," Dent concluded, "this is plain Rebellion."

The murders at Point Lookout only sharpened Fendall's conviction that a Catholic-Indian plot was afoot. John Bright, a landless farmer with a wife and four small children, was working for Fendall making fence rails, saving his earnings in hopes of purchasing land farther to the south.

"Stay but a little while here and there will be land enough for us all one of these daies," Fendall advised Bright.

"How can that be"?

"Why," said Fendall, "the King and Parliament in England are at warrs" over the Popish Plot. Once that was fully suppressed in England, Protestants would control the colonies as well. "So you need not fear," he told Bright. There would soon be land enough along the Potomac, at least for Protestants.[2]

The Iroquois arrived in force in June 1681, taking thirteen prisoners before the Piscataways could retreat to Zachia Swamp. Guided by the recently captured Mattawoman werowance, some of the northern raiders tore down fences and prevented the Piscataways from working their cornfields. Meanwhile twenty warriors, half of them Susuquehannocks, paddled all the way to the mouth of the Potomac "to hunt for other Indians." The Mattawomans among the besiegers shouted to the Piscataways in their palisaded town that their enemies were the Susquehannocks and Doegs. Two or three Frenchmen, they warned, were among them. Papists.

A few days later, British rangers under Captain Randolph Brandt visiting the fort stumbled upon a peace parley between the Piscataways and their besiegers. Brandt watched as the Piscataways and northerners spoke in turn, delivering gifts to seal each declaration. Later the parley moved to the main Iroquois encampment, where they spoke for another four hours. "Much friendship past betweene them," Brandt thought. When the Piscataways prepared to leave, however, the northerners seized them and led them away as prisoners. Brandt was allowed to leave, but he could not convince the invaders to negotiate with the English. That, the besiegers said, could wait until they had finished dealing with the Piscataways.

Brandt's rangers visited the Piscataway fort again six weeks later. As they approached they noticed that although all seemed quiet, the fort's gates were closed and Piscataway men had their guns at the ready. Suddenly, northern raiders "appeared in the Corne very neare the fort." The Piscataways fired several volleys past the Englishmen as the Iroquois found cover in the cornfield and returned fire. "I Doubt they were upon a treaty," Brandt wryly noted. The Piscataways called to him that there were at least 600 attackers, "and did advise me to come into the Fort." This struck Brandt as an excellent idea.

When Brandt awoke the next morning the northerners were gone, leaving a broad path of trampled ground and ruined cornfields leading off to the northwest from the Zachiah Fort. The Piscataways told Brandt that "had wee not come they [would have] been cutt off thatt night." Brandt wondered, though. Had he prevented the final destruction of the Piscataways, or had he prevented a Piscataway surrender and alliance with the northerners?[3]

Fendall interpreted the northern Indians' siege of the Piscataway fort as a sign that the grand plot was coming to fruition. Like an anti-Catholic Paul Revere he spread the alarm, sailing from plantation to plantation along the Potomac and its tributaries to rally Protestants against the popish-Indian conspirators. Soon joined by John Coode, he worked his way downriver to Nicholas Spencer's house, catching the secretary just as he returned from testifying on behalf of the canoe-makers for the Point Lookout murders. What should they do, Fendall and Coode asked Spencer, now that "the Papists and Indians were joined together"? Spencer refused to get directly involved, but did nothing to prevent them from resuming their travels and warning everyone they met to expect "to be cut off by the Indians and Papists together." If they acted soon, they assured their neighbors, they could still vanquish the Catholics. Soon, Coode promised, no "Papist" would "have one foote of land."

Upon the heels of this outburst, Lord Baltimore ordered the arrest of Fendall and Coode as "two Rank Baconists" who "have been tampering to stirr up the Inhabitants" to mutiny and meant to "possess themselves here and in Virginia of what estates they pleased." Virginians were "as ripe and readdy for another Rebellion as ever they were," Baltimore warned royal officials in England, but Virginia officials, he feared, were either oblivious to the danger or deliberately looking the other way.

Word of Fendall's and Coode's arrests spread quickly among their sympathizers. Nearly a dozen men were present at the home of George Godfrey, a planter, justice of the peace, and militia lieutenant in Fendall's county, when the news arrived on July 14. Another visitor, William Boyden, arrived a few minutes later to find Godfrey already recruiting a band of armed men to liberate Fendall. Boyden, though, convinced them that ten men would not be enough. Still determined to free Fendall, Godfrey decided to "goe to Church next Sonday, and gett what men he could there to joyne with those men he had already sent for to meete him in armes at Church."

Many parishioners arrived early that Sunday for Protestant services. The "generall discourse amongst the people there," one later recalled, was "that My Lord [Baltimore] had lett the Indians have powder and shott." Daniel Mathena contributed the story of an Indian with "a parcell of Letters in a silk grass basket" who had visited his house two years earlier. The letters, the Indian said, came from Lord Baltimore, and he was carrying them to the Iroquois. Mrs. Mathena asked why Baltimore would write letters, since the Iroquois couldn't read. The Indian explained that the French were nearby, and that they would read them.

A few churchgoers may have wondered why the Indian had volunteered so much information, or why Mathena had waited two years before telling his story, but to everyone else it made sense. The idea of a correspondence between English and French Catholics, carried by a local Indian who thought nothing of going into the Iroquois towns, fit perfectly with the stories told by Nathaniel Bacon, by the authors of the "Complaint from Heaven," and with a thousand other tales of conspiracies with the Indians that had been circulating since the rebellion.

Boyden, arriving late to church, found forty angry, frustrated men under arms but with nowhere to go. Fendall, they had learned, had been "remooved into St Maries County or elsewhere." Where, exactly, none could say. Forced to disband, they returned home and awaited the government's inevitable reaction. By early August it had arrived. Godfrey had been stripped of his offices, brought to the capital, and jailed pending trial alongside Fendall and Coode.[4]

The Provincial Court met in mid-November in the Assembly chamber of Maryland's new brick statehouse. The judges had a crowded docket of lawsuits and serious criminal cases to work through, but the people filling the inns and taverns of St. Mary's City particularly wanted to see the trials of Fendall, Coode, and Godfrey. Fendall, especially, was expected to mount an aggressive defense.

Godfrey went first, pleading not guilty to attempting to "sett [Fendall] at large to make Rebellious Insurrections." The trial raced along quickly: by the end of the day Godfrey had been convicted, and the following morning was sentenced to hang.

With that sentence still echoing through the courtroom, jury selection began in Fendall's trial. Representing himself, Fendall made no exception to any of the prospective Protestant jurors:

FENDALL: Are you a Catholick or a Protestant
ANTHONY DAWSON: I am a Protestant
FENDALL: I make no exceptions

Catholics were treated differently:

CL[ERK]: John Hungerford
HUNGERFORD: Here
FENDALL: What are you?
HUNGERFORD: I am not bound to tell

FENDALL: It is but a small request I desire to be satisfied.

HUNGERFORD: I am a Catholick

FENDALL: If you be a Roman Catholick I except against you.

HUNGERFORD: I am a Roman Catholick

COURT: He is dismissd

Using this simple test, Fendall managed to assemble an all-Protestant jury. He then proceeded to attack the parade of witnesses brought against him. William Boyden, he said, had asked him to raise a rebellion, promising to raise forty men himself. Now, Fendall scoffed, "fearing this might come in against him," Boyden "was resolved to prevent it by crying whore first and fathering his own Crimes upon others." Two more witnesses, John and Isabella Bright, held long-standing grudges against him, Fendall explained. Their testimony was therefore simply another way to "waylay" him. Still another witness was attacked for not having come forward earlier to report a conversation in which Fendall was said to have spoken treasonous words. Perhaps, said Fendall, it was because the witness had been the one to speak those words, and "has inverted the scene . . . to save himself."

The jury was not convinced. They retired only briefly before returning their verdict: "We find Josias Fendall guilty of speaking severall seditious words," though without actual "force or practice."

In the crowded warmth of the town's inns and taverns that evening, the curious debated Fendall's likely fate. He could not be put to death; unlike Godfrey he had not raised arms against the government. But he could have his tongue bored through and his ears cropped. Would the court go so far as that? The suspense vanished the following day, when the court sentenced Fendall to pay a fine of 40,000 pounds of tobacco (the equivalent of at least twenty-five tobacco workers' production for an entire year) and banished him from the province forever.

Coode's trial, later that same day, came as an anticlimax. There would be no death sentence, no bored tongue or cropped ears, not even a banishment. Fendall's accomplice was found not guilty of sedition. He was free to go—after a lecture. "Let me give you some advice," offered Lord Baltimore's cousin Phillip Calvert. "Keepe a Guard upon your Tongue. [Y]ou love to amaze the Ignorant and make sport with your witt." Such jesting about serious matters had given people good reason to suspect that "you were of the same tribe with Fendall," especially since "you were observed then to visit one another and make visits to others."

Baltimore dispatched transcripts of the trials to the king's Privy Council, both to counteract his opponents' accusations against his government and to warn them that the danger of another uprising had not yet passed. "Had not these three persons been secured in time," he asserted, "you would soon have heard of another Bacon." Indeed, Fendall might yet turn out to assume the role of that second Bacon. He had moved to Virginia, where he seemed "the mostly likely person" to rally the "discontented party . . . to stirr upp another rebellion." Cautious of stirring up a rebellion himself, Baltimore pardoned Godfrey rather than hanging him and making him a martyr.[5]

The "rebellion," when it came, broke out first in Gloucester County in the spring of 1682. The fields were already dotted with tobacco plants sprouting from freshly hoed mounds. But some

Gloucester planters had already decided that "noe Tobaccos should bee this year planted." So much had been grown, they complained, that prices had sunk too low for planters to make a living. One Burgess had been heard to say the previous spring that if the government refused to take steps to limit production "wee must all goe a plundering." Hopeful that restricting the supply of tobacco would raise its price, the Burgesses were "big with expectation to enact a Cessation" of tobacco production at the upcoming Assembly. When the legislators arrived in Jamestown in April, though, they learned that Thomas Culpeper, who had been appointed governor in 1677 but had spent only three months in the colony since then, had ordered acting governor Henry Chicheley to postpone the Assembly until November. Culpeper was at last en route to Virginia, and he wanted to preside over the Assembly himself.

News of the Assembly's postponement arrived along with a message from Charles II, responding to the Burgesses' concerns about the restless remnants of the troops that had been sent to put down Bacon's Rebellion five years earlier. Charles offered a choice: the troops might either be continued in service but paid by Virginia's taxpayers, or disbanded. Since it was already mid-April Chicheley decided to allow the Burgesses to meet for the limited purpose of deciding this issue, while otherwise honoring Culpeper's order to adjourn.

Virginia, the Assembly quickly decided, could not afford to pay for the Regulars any longer. The troops were disbanded. The Burgesses, however, found this issue less interesting than the moratorium on tobacco production. In defiance of the order to discuss only the fate of the Regulars, Robert Beverley took the floor and argued vociferously for a one-year cession on tobacco-planting. Chicheley hastily shut down the debate and sent the legislators home, but by then it was too late: Beverly had already "instilled into the multitude" a justification for "making a Cessation by cutting up of plants." The Burgesses left Jamestown on April 27, spreading their dissatisfaction with the government's inaction along the roads and rivers that carried them home.

Since the Assembly could not act, the Gloucester men decided that they would. On May 1 a band of twenty-two men went into their own fields and destroyed thousands of young tobacco plants. From there they went from farm to farm cutting down plants. Chicheley was still in Jamestown, meeting with the Council, when word of the tobacco-cutting arrived. Councilor Matthew Kemp, commander of the Gloucester militia, quickly saddled up and rode home, called out the militia, and surprised the tobacco-cutters in the act.

Yet arresting the leaders of the Gloucester riots failed to stop the revolt. Night after night the destruction of tobacco plants continued, spreading inland to New Kent County and northward to the Potomac. All of the county militias were called up, but by the end of the month, Chicheley estimated, three-quarters of the Gloucester tobacco crop had been ruined (often by women who picked up where the men had left off after their arrest). Half of New Kent's plants and part of the crops in three other counties were also spoiled.

Virginia's government prosecuted the plant-cutters' leaders as traitors, hanging two of them in front of crowds gathered for county court sessions in Jamestown and Gloucester County. Baltimore agreed that it had been treason, writing that the plant-cutters were "tending very much to the same design of that of the late rebell there Bacon." Secretary Spencer too blamed the "spirit of Rebellion, to which too many of the Inhabitants have an Itching desire, since the late Rebellion."

The readiness to discern Bacon's influence in the plant-cutting riots was testimony that his rebellion had not yet been put to rest. Nor would it be, so long as substantial numbers of planters and servants, full of expectations but frustrated by economic realities, stood ready to blame Indians and the provincial government for their inability to establish themselves as planters and patriarchs.[6]

Like many planters, William Byrd was short of laborers in the 1680s. Times had improved in England, so with each passing year fewer young men and women were willing to come to America as indentured servants. Virginians had long since realized that enslaved Africans were the most profitable laborers, and most wealthy planters owned at least a few slaves, but they were still hard to come by. "I understande there are some Negro Ships expected into York now every day," wrote one planter, but "before I can have notice, they'll be all dispos'd of."

Byrd acquired whatever sort of laborer came to hand: servants or slaves, English or African. Indian slaves filled out his labor force, and he sold more Indians acquired through the Piedmont trade to other colonists. Ordinary planters, lacking Byrd's wealth and trading connections, relied especially heavily on Indian slaves. On the upper James 40 percent of the slaves were Indians, not Africans, and they were concentrated in the hands of nonelite planters. This was especially true of enslaved children, who would end up serving the longest terms: when a 1680 statute required counties to register the ages of young slaves for purposes of taxation, the Henrico County court recorded thirty-three Indian children and no "negros"; in other counties, between one-half and one-third of those recorded were Indians.[7]

With indentured servitude slowly giving way to slavery, planters needed to tighten their control over laborers. At the November 1682 session of the Assembly the Burgesses, meeting in William Arminger's newly built Jamestown tavern amid the collapsed walls, crumbling foundations, and charred beams of the buildings burned in 1676, passed an "act for the better preventing insurrections by Negroes." Eager to close any legal loopholes that might allow Africans and Indians to gain their freedom, the Burgesses ruled that Africans and other "servants not being christians" imported by sea were invariably to be considered slaves, while Indians captured by Virginia's Native allies and then sold to the English were "slaves to all intents and purposes, any law, usage or custome to the contrary notwithstanding." Even Indians fortunate enough to be servants rather than slaves had to serve a minimum of twelve years or until they turned thirty, whichever came later—far longer terms than were required of white indentured servants.[8]

The colonists' deepening involvement in the Indian slave trade coincided with interruptions in both provinces' leadership. Baltimore left Maryland to defend his interests in London, leaving his Council member and business manager Henry Darnall in charge. Baltimore had acquired a rival in the well-connected William Penn, whose new colony of Pennsylvania (1681) bordered

Maryland on the north. Already the two proprietors were embroiled in a boundary dispute. Baltimore also needed to be in London to combat the continuing stream of accusations that his government discriminated against Protestants. He sailed for England in the spring of 1684.

Virginia too suffered from turnover at the top. Governor Culpeper sailed for England in May 1683, having spent just six months at his post. The king, surprised to see him back so soon, stripped Culpeper of the governorship and sent in his place Francis Howard, Baron Howard of Effingham. Nearly two years passed between Culpeper's departure and Effingham's arrival; in the meantime, Nicholas Spencer served as acting governor.

When he finally arrived in Virginia in February 1684, Effingham made his home at Thomas Pate's Gloucester Hall (perhaps unknowingly passing over Bacon's unmarked grave while out walking or exercising his horse). Effingham soon resolved to do something about the ongoing Iroquois attacks. As soon as the spring Assembly session ended he sailed for New York, partly to visit his friend Thomas Dongan, who had recently replaced Edmund Andros as governor there, and partly to travel up the Hudson River "on a hopefull prospect of Settling a firme and lasting Peace" with the Five Nations. When he returned to Jamestown in the early autumn, he carried with him a renewal of Coursey's 1677 treaty that he believed would end "those dayly Alarams and Mischeifs Virginia hath received from its troublesom Indian Neighbors."[9]

Charles II arose early on Monday, February 2, 1685, after a bad night's sleep. At about 7 A.M., as he was leaving his chambers after "his private Devotions," he collapsed in what those present called a "fit of apoplexy." Doctors swarmed in. They immediately bled sixteen ounces from him, and when that failed to revive him they drew another eight ounces of blood from cuts across his shoulders. Emetics made him vomit, and enemas emptied his bowels. Nothing worked, not even blistering his shaved head with a hot iron, applying plasters to his feet, or giving him sneezing powders and laxatives. When Charles took a turn for the worse on Wednesday the doctors pulled out all the stops, feeding him the powdered skull of a man who had never been buried, and bezoars, powdered stones from a goat's intestines. On Thursday night a priest was secretly admitted to the king's bedside to accept his conversion to Catholicism and administer the last rites. Charles died the following morning, leaving to his Catholic brother James the throne of an aggressively Protestant nation.[10]

James could count himself fortunate that his brother had died at fifty-five and not earlier. In the several years since the panic over the Popish Plot Charles II had pacified Parliament by allying himself with the Tory Party, gaining their loyal support by advancing their policies and by convincing them that pushing to exclude James from the throne and agitating about the Popish Plot would subvert the established order and plunge England into the chaos of civil war. Together Charles II and his Tory allies took their case to the people, deftly organizing a public relations campaign depicting their opponents as dangerous radicals and appointing like-minded men to the realm's thousands of unglamorous but critically important frontline positions in local government.

It also helped that James and his Catholic wife Mary, married since 1673, had no living children in 1685. James was already fifty-one. When James died the throne would pass to his eldest daughter Mary or her younger sister Anne, children from an earlier marriage who had been raised as Protestants. Better still, Mary's husband was William of Orange, a Dutch military commander who had emerged as the leading defender of Protestant Europe against the French. Those who worried about James's Catholicism found his orderly succession to the throne at least palatable as long as they could look forward to the day, not so far off, when his Protestant daughter and her Dutch husband would rule England. William and Mary, at least, could be counted upon to deploy England's power against Louis XIV's popish tyranny and arbitrary rule.

There was, however, a rival claimant to the throne. Charles had elevated his eldest illegitimate son to the peerage, naming him the Duke of Monmouth, and had given him command of England's land forces in 1678. The handsome (and Protestant) Monmouth had emerged as a popular choice as heir among those who wanted to prevent James from inheriting the throne, and he did little to discourage them. Almost inevitably, Monmouth was implicated in a plot against his uncle James and forced to flee to the Low Countries in 1683.

In the wake of his father's death Monmouth returned to claim the throne, landing in the west of England and recruiting an army as he marched toward London. The decisive battle came on the night of June 5, 1685, when Monmouth launched a surprise attack on James's outnumbered army. Monmouth's inexperienced force lost the element of surprise early on, fired prematurely, and broke ranks when James's army launched its counter-assault. A third of Monmouth's men were cut down as they fled. Hundreds more were executed in the following weeks, died in jail, or were sentenced to ten years of hard labor in the West Indies. Monmouth, found hiding in a ditch, was executed before a large London crowd. The executioner botched the job, taking five blows to sever the rebel's head. Somehow, though, the rumor spread that Monmouth was alive and would one day return to topple his uncle from the throne.[11]

Effingham had worried ever since his arrival that unrepentant Baconites were simply biding their time, awaiting the right moment to rise again. Monmouth's Rebellion was obviously such an occasion, for the pretender had long had a following in Virginia. During Bacon's Rebellion, stories had circulated that the rebels "need not fear the king, nor any force out of England . . . for the king was dead and the people together by the ears & the Duke of York and the Duke of Monmouth fighting." Now, in 1685, colonists eagerly embraced rumors that Monmouth's Rebellion had succeeded or that Monmouth was still at large. Such tales, Effingham wrote, "so farr Imboldened some that their Tongues runn at Large and Demonstrated the wickedness of their harts." Even among the Burgesses "the Courage, or rather Impudence, that some of them take from the last Rebellion of Monmouth," was evident. If not for the quick suppression of the uprising, Effingham added, "I could not have given so good an Account of the Quietnesse of this place."[12]

Josias Fendall died in northern Virginia in 1687, not far from where the killing of the herdsman Robert Hen had set in motion the events leading Bacon's Rebellion. The death of this leading "Baconist," however, did nothing to change the opinions that had led so many to follow Bacon and his successors as leaders of the populist revolt. Indeed, reports from the end of 1687 warned that Virginia and Maryland were "ripe for disturbances" by people who would "be very apt to pretend religion the better to carry on their evill Designs."[13]

Cockacoeske, too, passed away in 1687. Contrary to colonists' fantasies casting the neighbor Indians as dangerous enemies working to destroy the province from within, the regal Cocka-coeske left behind a Pamunkey nation that had fallen on difficult times. Her people were equally vulnerable to the depredations of Iroquois raiders and those of neighboring colonists. They were in no condition to oppose the English. The chieftaincy passed to Cockacoeske's niece, "Ms. Betty," who, tellingly, scarcely merited attention in Virginia's records.[14]

# Ten

# TALES OF A REVOLUTION

❦

WILLIAM BYRD SPENT THE WINTER OF 1688–1689 IN THE usual way, staying close to home at the falls of the James River to supervise the processing and packaging of his tobacco, skins, and furs and writing letters to his English business associates to be carried to England by the spring fleet. The opportunities to gather news and post letters to England were fewer than usual that season because fewer ships were coming into port: rumors of war with both the Dutch and the French meant that English ships were wary about venturing across the Atlantic. And the news that did come was so alarming that Byrd could bring himself to write of it only in the most general, politically neutral terms. "I am heartily sorry to hear of the troubles with you," he wrote one of his London agents in late January. "Pray God give a good issue to them."[1]

Byrd was responding to the first reports of an upheaval in England. William of Orange, James's Dutch son-in-law, had issued a declaration in October announcing plans to invade England with a force sufficient for "the preservation of the Protestant Religion, the covering of all men from persecution for their conscience, and the securing to the whole nation the free enjoyment of all their laws, rights, and liberties, under a just and legal government."[2]

James II had come to the throne in 1685 intending to make his fellow Catholics' lives easier while also trying to assure his subjects that his policy of religious tolerance would include Protestants of all descriptions. But these assurances made the already suspicious populace more alert than ever for signs of creeping "popery," while also alienating the religiously orthodox Tory allies his brother had bequeathed him. James's fidelity to the alliance his brother Charles had forged with Louis XIV in 1668 also upset his subjects, who increasingly favored closer relations with France's Protestant Dutch enemies. Then, early in 1688, James II withdrew three English regiments that had long been stationed on the Continent to protect the Dutch Republic against France, sending exactly the wrong signal to his wary subjects.

Worse, on June 10, 1688, the king's consort Maria gave birth to a son—a Catholic heir to the throne. The bonfires, fireworks, balloon launchings, and days of thanksgiving that James II ordered seemed horribly off-key. Far from being a cause for celebration, the prospect of an unbroken Catholic dynasty of English kings "gave the greatest agonys imaginable to the generality of the Kingdom." Many people eagerly circulated the story that the infant was really someone else's baby who had been smuggled into the queen's chambers to be passed off as James's legitimate heir.

Three weeks later, seven prominent members of the nobility, church, and military wrote William of Orange that the English people were "so generally dissatisfied with the present conduct of the government in relation to their religion, liberties and properties . . . that your Highness may be assured there are nineteen parts of twenty of the people throughout the kingdom who are desirous of a change." If William could land a credible force in England, they assured him, sailors, soldiers, and citizens would rise up.[3]

William landed on Guy Fawkes Day, November 5, 1688, a major national holiday celebrating the thwarting of a Catholic plot in 1605 to blow up Parliament and the royal family. As William's army marched toward London the king suffered a series of humiliating defections, including John Churchill, a lifelong friend who had led the army to victory over Monmouth in 1685. Sir John Berry also declared for William—the same Berry who had led the naval squadron sent to suppress Bacon's Rebellion. Many Protestant naval officers came with him. Even the king's daughter Anne, in line for the throne after her sister Mary, slipped away.

The queen, disguised as a laundrywoman, fled to France with her infant son on December 10. James boarded a vessel for France the following night, but was caught and returned to London with a military escort. William, anxious to avoid having to imprison or execute the king, quietly arranged for James's next "escape," providing transportation and a military escort that looked the other way when he sailed for France on December 23. A new Parliament convened in January to decide how to proceed in the absence of James II, and William was formally offered the throne in a public ceremony on February 13, 1689.

A week later, Lord Baltimore sent a messenger to Maryland ordering that William and Mary be proclaimed king and queen.

A duplicate order went out several days later. Baltimore's messenger, however, died before sailing from England. The duplicate order, too, miscarried—or, it was later charged, was ignored.[4]

In the absence of news from England, provincial governors proceeded as if James were still king. Baltimore's deputy in Maryland, Council member William Joseph, addressed the new Assembly in St. Mary's City on November 14, nine days after William landed in England. His voice echoing from the brick walls of the Assembly chamber, Joseph lectured his audience on the divine right of kings and called for an annual day of thanksgiving celebrating the birth of the Prince of Wales. In Virginia, news of the Prince of Wales's birth caught up with Governor Effingham while he was visiting on the Rappahannock River. It was impossible to obtain a quorum of the Council so far from Jamestown, but Effingham made do by summoning three councilors who lived nearby to issue a call for a day of thanksgiving.

Effingham had been begging James II to recall him for the past two years. In late February, still unaware of the king's flight to France, he called one last meeting with the Council at Jamestown and announced to his startled councilors that he was going home and leaving the Council to govern until a replacement arrived. The departure, exquisitely timed, saved Effingham a world of trouble. By the time the Council reconvened on April 19, they faced an epidemic of "falce and Extravigant reports" that there was no longer any "King, Laws nor Government" in place. Virginia's councilors were papists, people were saying, and the Catholics "had hired the Indyans to assist them to Cutt of[f] all the Protestants." Ten thousand Iroquois and 9,000 Eastern Shore

Indians were massing for an attack. Panicked Virginians had begun "drawing themselves into parties with force of Armes." As in the spring of 1676, drumbeats sounded through the woods calling up volunteers to defend against the invaders.

The Council was packed with men who had learned the lessons of Bacon's Rebellion well. Unlike the Council of 1676 they reacted decisively to the rumors, which they regarded as mere pretexts to "Stirr up and Carry on a Rebellion." They immediately proclaimed William and Mary king and queen. In a hastily arranged ceremony in front of the Jamestown courthouse on April 27, the sheriff drummed up a crowd on short notice to witness the "fireing [of] Great Guns, Sounding of Trumpetts and beating of Drums."

Meanwhile, warrants went out for the arrest of seven "Notorious Actors in those Rebellious and Outragious Actings." Avoiding Berkeley's mistakes with Bacon, the Council neither made martyrs of the "Actors" nor allowed them to go completely free. Instead the culprits had to post extremely high bonds for their good behavior and were ordered to appear at the October session of the General Court. George Mason, a Stafford County magistrate and militia officer accused of supporting the rebels, was suspended from office. The home of Giles Brent, a Catholic, was searched for weapons in order to discredit rumors that he was hoarding arms to be used against the Protestants, and he was forced to move into the home of a fellow magistrate, the reliably loyalist William Fitzhugh, to show that the provincial government was keeping an eye on him.[5]

In northern Virginia and Maryland tales of invasions and betrayals multiplied: that Indians on the Eastern Shore, letting down their guard while drinking, had said "that they were hyred . . . to fight against the English"; that 10,000 Iroquois warriors had built a fort at the head of the Potomac; that the fort was actually on a different river or possibly at Baltimore's Mattapany estate; that Catholics in the government had seized the militias' arms and ammunition so that Protestants could not defend themselves; that the Piscataways and other neighbor Indians were part of the plot; that rebels from Virginia were about to invade Maryland; that Virginians were going to help rescue Maryland's Protestants; that the Dutch were coming down with the Iroquois; that the invaders were coming by land and that they would come by sea.

With so many people repeating these rumors, it seemed, there had to be something to them. Maryland's Colonel Henry Jowles, who had suppressed the Affair at the Clifts during Bacon's Rebellion, certainly thought so. The papers from Virginia, he wrote his fellow militia colonel William Diggs, prove that "wee are sold and betrayed to the heathen" by the government itself. Most of the Council was implicated in the plot, Jowles believed, and the Indians were nearly ready to attack. Clearly it was "high time to be doeing something." He urged Diggs "to Espouse the protestant interest"; if he did, "the whole Country you may be assured will faithfully stand by you."

Jowles begged for a speedy answer, and indeed Diggs scrawled a reply the same day. But rather than accept the offer to lead an uprising against the government, Diggs wrote, he was on his way to Mattapany to show Jowles's letter to the Council. The councilors appreciated Jowles's warning and, at Diggs's suggestion, promised to return the weapons taken from the militia storehouses to be used however Jowles thought best. They encouraged him to "goe to the head of the River" to see for himself if "those heathen people or any others are found in open Armes against the English." If so, the Council authorized him to attack.

Jowles was no Josias Fendall or John Coode. He willingly accepted the Council's orders to meet with the Indians before acting, and even allowed a Catholic Council member and militia colonel, Henry Darnall, to address his troops. As Darnall described the scene, however, there were "a great many of the people Assembled in Armes" who refused to disperse upon his orders alone. It didn't help that other messengers counteracted his reassurances "with very false Rumours." More disturbingly, some spoke of "sending for the Virginians to come to their assistance." The crowd dispersed only after Colonel Diggs, a Protestant, arrived and added his assurances to Darnall's.

But would they stay dispersed? Was it too late to prevent the Virginians from intervening? Diggs and Jowles sent a boat across the river to Nicholas Spencer's home, "desireing him to undeceave the people" of Virginia "and use his assistance against such insurrections." At the end of what was already a very long day, Diggs sailed again to the Council at Mattapany while Jowles and Darnall led a troop of horses to search for Indians "to further satisfy the people" that they were safe.

Jowles found no traces of an Indian invasion. Nor did Darnall, nor Brandt's rangers, nor any of the half-dozen parties sent out to investigate. Even at the Clifts, a hotbed of anti-Proprietary sentiment, searchers concluded that "the late feares and disturbances raised concerning nine thousand Indians French and papists . . . is utterly false." Certainly there was "noe designe of any plott Contrivance or Conspiracy" by the government itself.

Exactly how these wild rumors had started in the first place remained something of a mystery. Tellingly, though, no one seemed surprised at the *contents* of these stories, or that so many people had been prepared to believe them. In truth, the bigger surprise was that Maryland's Council had not yet had the wits to proclaim William and Mary their new monarchs.[6]

Virginians and Marylanders had to guess at what was happening on the other side of the Atlantic in the spring of 1689. James II had fled to France, and William could be counted on to bring Britain into his Dutch war with France, the most powerful nation in Europe. That much they knew. But how would England fare in that war? With French aid, could James dislodge William from the throne? And could French and Indian attacks on the British colonies be far behind?

John Coode thought not. The recent panic over a popish-Indian plot, he was convinced, had been premature but not misplaced. New rumors circulated that the government had confiscated the militia's arms under the pretence of repairing them, and that the Catholics had been bragging about "the French King's Invincible Army." Coode began to recruit members to an extralegal "Protestant Association" whose purpose was to "preserve, vindicate and assert the sovereign Dominion and right of King William and Queen Mary" in America against the "destruction, that is plotted and designed" by English Catholics in league with the French and Indians.

Weeks passed, and then months, and still Maryland's Council did not acknowledge the new monarchs. As May turned into June and June into July, suspicions mounted that the councilors were deliberately suppressing their orders from England. Coode's Protestant Associators gained momentum with each passing day. The perception grew that "the overruling hand of Divine Providence" was "opening our eyes to discern our Duty" to demand that the provincial government acknowledge William and Mary.

The Council's failure to declare for the new king and queen caused outrage, but not surprise. More than a decade of rumors and unrest had convinced many people that for men such as Berkeley and Baltimore, Indian alliances were the key to establishing "french Despotick" rule. Since the rebellion, the situation had only become clearer and the stakes larger. Whereas Bacon had believed that he could look to Charles II to save Virginia from its governor and Indians, his successors had to reckon with the "danger," as Coode explained, "of being undermined and betrayed by the hopes and encouragement [of] the papists"— including the king. And now, what could the Catholic-dominated Council possibly be waiting for, if not for the arrival of their French and Indian allies?

A repeat of 1681 was about to unfold, predicted the Associators, with French Jesuits coordinating the northern Indians' offensive while Baltimore exploited the crisis to wield "an unlimited and tyrannicall power." Confronted by this potent coalition, the Associators prayed that help would come soon from "our neighbour Collony of Virginia, from whose friendshipp, vicinity great loyalty and samenes of Religion wee may expect assistance in our greatest necessity."[7]

Colonel Darnall was with the Council at Mattapany on July 16. "The Country was all quiet, no appearance of any Enemy," Indian or rebel, he reported. Mattapany was well-secured, guarded by 300 provincial troops, and nearby St. Mary's City had been transformed into a garrison under Colonel Diggs.

Late that night a messenger arrived with news that Coode was raising troops at his home near St. Mary's, distributing arms to his followers as they came in. Was it true? It was hard to tell with so many rumors swirling about. Darnall convened the Council, which sent an agent to find out. This time, they learned, the story was true—though there was no confirmation of it for two days because the councilors' scout was "taken by Coode as a spy."

The Council members' isolation at Mattapany allowed a new round of tales to fill the silence along the Potomac. On the paths and waterways planters met and passed along the word that the "Papists" had "invited the Northern Indians to come down and cutt off the Protestants." The Indians were already gathering and would arrive "about the latter end of August when roasting Eares were in season." Coode and his fellow Associators planned a pre-emptive attack to seize the magazines at St. Mary's and Mattapany, remove the "Papists" from power, prepare a vigorous defense against the Indian invasion, and "proclaim the King and Queen." By July 18 they were marching toward St. Mary's, adding to their army as they went. Entire militia units had already joined Coode—including, ominously, Colonel Jowles.

Darnall headed in the opposite direction, going north of St. Mary's to raise men against Coode. Many officers were prepared to follow orders, he reported, but the men in the ranks of the militia refused to fight. Employing the same logic as the Gloucester militia had in 1676, they believed that Coode intended "only to preserve the Country from the Indians and Papists and to proclaim the King and Queen." In the end barely 150 answered Darnall's call to arms. It was too little, and too late. Coode's army, swollen to 700 men, had already arrived at St. Mary's.

Most of St. Mary's lay open to Coode's troops, but the port-holes and windows of the statehouse bristled with the gun barrels of Diggs's men. Coode, gambling that the defenders would be reluctant to fight, advanced his men to "less then within Pistolll shot." No shots were fired as Coode sent in a messenger carrying a written declaration of the Protestant Association's case, demanding it be read aloud so that all of Diggs's men might hear it. Coode insisted that they surrender the statehouse, their arms, and the colony's records "to their Majesty's use." As Coode had antici-pated, Diggs's real problem was convincing his own men that they were fighting on the right side. Eighty defenders refused to defend the statehouse. Diggs was forced to surrender the capital without firing a shot.

The fall of St. Mary's was a serious blow, but the Council hoped that the numbers would be less lopsided at Mattapany. Darnall had already rallied 300 defenders, and new recruiting parties went out to the northern counties. To those unwilling "to fight for the papists against themselves," at least one officer successfully argued that "it was not religion but the settled peace, Govern-ment and Lawes of the Land" that were at stake. To those who assumed that Coode had authority from England for his actions, the officer replied that "you may be sure they have none, for if they could produce any such thing" they would have displayed it. More men, a majority of them Protestant, joined the loyalist gar-rison at Mattapany.

The Council, meanwhile, tried to persuade Jowles to change sides. In March he had thrown his weight toward the Council, working tirelessly to investigate and debunk tales of an imminent French and Indian attack. The rumors this time were nearly identical. Could not the truth win over Jowles again? Another messenger traversed the narrow peninsula between Mattapany and St. Mary's, bearing an offer to make Jowles "General of all the Forces in the Province." This time, however, Jowles recommitted to Coode. Desperate, the Council issued a proclamation pardoning the rebels if they laid down their arms and went home, but Coode would not read it to his men. Instead he forged a different message from the Council, "a dyfyance from Us, whereby to enrage and not pacify them." The Council could do little more: they had lost their two leading Protestant officers, Diggs and Jowles, gained but few new troops, and decisively lost the propaganda war.

When Coode arrived at Mattapany Darnall sent out a message asking him to conduct negotiations within hearing of the rebel army. "If we could but obtain that in the hearing of the People," Darnall still hoped, "we should be able to disabuse them, and clear ourselves of what they were made to believe against us." Coode, however, had nothing to gain by this. Rather than give the councilors a forum, he spread a rumor within his army that "that our neighbour Indians had cut up their Corn and were gone from their Towns" in preparation for war. Mattapany's Protestant defenders, he told the councilors, must be allowed to leave, for surely they were being detained there against their wills. Mattapany itself must surrender upon the terms he dictated, or else Coode would "proceed to storm itt." With "no hope left of quieting or repelling the People thus enraged," Darnall and his loyalists had no choice but to surrender their arms, the proprietor's residence, and control of the government.

All that was left for Coode to accomplish now was to avoid hanging.[8]

· *Eleven* ·

# Bacon's Heirs

NATHANIEL BACON'S VOLUNTEERS HAD LOST THE FIRST round of the rebellion in 1676–1677, but their diagnosis of Virginia's problems lived on. The virulent anti-popery that emerged in the latter stages of Bacon's Rebellion kept the cause alive, elevating it the level of a struggle between God (through Protestantism and the English nation) and Satan (through the pope, the French, the Jesuits, and the Indians). Others, culminating in Coode, had inherited Bacon's leadership of the movement. But would their story end on the same unhappy note? Overthrowing the governor and Council, after all, was not the same thing as establishing a functioning new government or winning the full support of the populace, let alone that of the king.

The key, always, was to control how the story was told. Coode's tale was essentially an elaboration on Bacon's. Like Bacon, he claimed to have raised the countryside against Indians when the governor refused to act in a time of crisis; then, upon discovering that the governor and his cronies had conspired with the Indians and against the people, he had (again like Bacon) taken control of his colony in the name of the king. In short, each presented his rebellion as fulfilling the king's desire for good government by ejecting a corrupt governor and Council who had pursued their own narrow interests rather than the interests of those they served.

Unlike Bacon, Coode got away with it.

Coode sent the first accounts of the uprising to England via a ship anchored near Mattapany. He forbade the captain from carrying any messages from loyalists. Letters presenting Coode's rebellion as part of William and Mary's Glorious Revolution (for so the events in England came to be known) went out to adjoining colonies, and a "Committee of Secrecy" was formed to investigate the proprietary government. The committee's findings, "that the late popish Governors" had "designed by several villanous practises and machinations to betray their Majestie's Protestant Subjects of this Province to the French, Northern and other Indians," were rushed to England.

Coode also took the precaution of governing lightly, avoiding making decisions lest one of them turn the king against him. He acted as governor under the title of commander in chief, implying that his role was merely transitional and that his motives were thus unselfish. The new Assembly that he convened also launched few initiatives that might risk displeasing the king. Stripping Catholics of political power seemed safe enough; it was no more than William had done. But anything more, even attacking the Indians who were allegedly about to destroy the colonists, might be seen as contrary to the king's interest.

Repeatedly frustrated in their efforts to find passage to England, loyalist refugees were unable to tell their version of the story to Crown officials until December. By then it was far too late. "We have thought fitt . . . to signify our Royall approbation of your having proclaimed Us and the Queen," William informed Coode's provisional government in February 1690, "and we do further authorize and impower you to continue in our name your care in the administration of the Government." Baltimore was stripped of his authority to govern Maryland, and Catholics were barred from holding office.[1]

As a teenage immigrant from London in the late 1660s William Byrd had sought his fortune on Virginia's far frontier, roaming the woods and learning Indian languages as he apprenticed in his uncle's Indian trade. By 1689 he had long since become a successful tobacco planter, ship owner, and member of the Council, but he remained a resident of Henrico County, an Indian trader, and militia captain. During the 1690s, however, Byrd turned away from the frontier and toward the Atlantic.

The shift came at least partly in response to the fallout from the Glorious Revolution. "Wee here can expect no setled times," Byrd mused, "till England is in peace." The Council's quick response to William and Mary's assumption of the throne had averted the kind of turmoil experienced by Maryland—and for that matter the rebellions in New York and the New England colonies, where the Revolution had opened the way for colonial rebellions against James II's appointed governors. But thanks to William's victory the French posed a more direct threat than ever. They would almost certainly take the war to America. If the French could draw the Iroquois into their side of the struggle, then Virginia would not be safe—especially on the frontier. "The colony might be able to "indure a small incursion now and then from the Indians alone," Byrd calculated, provided "the French come not with them."

Economic circumstances also led Byrd to shift the focus of his activities closer to Jamestown. During William's war with France (1689–1697) fewer merchant ships came to Virginia than before. Those that did could fill their holds with cargo without having to come very far upriver. Byrd began shipping his goods from a new plantation, called Westover, twenty miles closer to Jamestown than his original home, and advertised that it lay but two miles above the place where the biggest deepwater ships anchored. A government appointment at Jamestown also drew him downriver. Pushed by his concerns about his family's safety at the falls and pulled by his business activities, Byrd sent all but the youngest of his children to be educated in England, further shifted his investments toward shipping and even the African slave trade, and made Westover his primary residence.[2]

Virginia's new lieutenant governor, Francis Nicholson, hated rebellion. A Yorkshireman who at twenty-two had entered the king's service in the Holland Regiment, Nicholson fought alongside the Dutch against French troops between 1678 and 1680. After further adventures in North Africa and Europe, he returned to England in time to lead troops in the climactic battle of Monmouth's Rebellion. In 1687 James II appointed Nicholson lieutenant governor for New York within the Dominion of New England, a newly created administrative union of the New England colonies and New York. Just as James II was expelled from England in 1688, so too was Nicholson chased from the Dominion in May 1689 by Leisler's Rebellion, New York's local variation on the Glorious Revolution. Returning to England, he managed to convince crown officials of his loyalty to the new monarchs and was rewarded with the lieutenant governorship of Virginia. It was to be a long stay: Nicholson alternated between the governorships of Virginia and Maryland throughout the 1690s and into the new century.[3]

Still smarting from his ejection from New York, Nicholson arrived in Virginia in May 1690 determined to wipe out the "leprosy of Rebellion which did so soon overspread all the Colonyes" during the Glorious Revolution. "The ignorant and fractious mob . . . only pleased in disorder and tumult," he believed. Although Virginians were "a very Cunning People," Nicholson bragged, "I not only baffled them, but got things past contrary to their Interest." Those measures included tighter enforcement of trade regulations, greater autonomy for the governor in military affairs, a stronger military presence on the frontier, and greater support for the Church of England.

Even those who had taken up arms in William's name against James II disgusted Nicholson. This created some discomfort when the governor was reassigned to Maryland in 1692 to make way for the former New York governor Edmund Andros to take over in Virginia (Andros stayed until 1698). It meant nothing to Nicholson that Coode and the Protestant Associators had rebelled on behalf of William and Mary, reported one observer: he "calls them Rebells," threatening "to hang them with Magna Charta about their necks." Nicholson took back powers for the governor that under Baltimore had belonged to the Assembly or local courts, then suppressed the inevitable complaints on the grounds that

"All Rebellions were begun in all Kingdomes and States by scandalizeing and makeing odious the persons in authority . . . as for Instance the late rebellion in Virginia by Bacon."

Yet the heirs of Bacon liked Nicholson. They had long sought to be governed more directly by the king and had often wished for a military-minded governor who would protect them from Indians, French tyranny, and popish plots. They preferred a governor who looked beyond his inner circle to consider the needs of county-level elites and ordinary planters, who could somehow keep the mass of ex-servants and other struggling small planters in line, and who shared their ideas about race, slavery, and Indians.

Nicholson was their man. Among his first acts were a tour of the frontier fortifications, a reform of the militia, and a move to establish permanent troops of frontier rangers. The governor took an unusually active role in defense: "On Rumours of danger, comotions or accidents," wrote one Virginian, "he is soon on the place in person." At home he kept an open table, entertaining nightly and taking pains to invite a steady stream of Burgesses to dinner. Conspicuously pious, he promoted the recruitment of more and better Church of England clergymen. He also hatched a plan for a college at Middle Plantation, to be supported by both English bishops and county fund-raising committees. The college, wisely named after William and Mary, was chartered in 1693. Construction quickly began on an impressive brick building that combined English and Dutch architectural styles in a way that seemed especially appropriate in the wake of the Glorious Revolution. In Maryland, too, Nicholson worked to strengthen the Church of England, going so far as to transfer the seat of government in 1694 from largely Catholic St. Mary's City to a Protestant stronghold farther north. He named the new capital Annapolis after James II's Protestant daughter Anne, now the childless William and Mary's heir to the throne. Soon a new statehouse, council house, church, prison, and a school named after William were under construction.[4]

Nicholson was transferred back to Virginia in 1698. Crown officials expected him to live in Jamestown, but after a fire burned down the recently rebuilt statehouse complex Nicholson decided to move the seat of government to a new capital at Middle Plantation. The Burgesses acquiesced, and once again Nicholson busied himself overseeing the procurement of bricks and a thousand other matters for the construction of a massive new capitol building in a Dutch-influenced style. Anne's ascension to the throne upon King William's death in 1702 (Mary had died of smallpox in 1694) provided Nicholson with still more opportunities to link Virginia's new seat of government to the empire. To the new capitol building he affixed a plaque on which "at top there was cut the Sun, Moon, and the planet Jupiter, and underneath thus HER MAJESTY QUEEN ANNE HER ROYALL CAPITOLL." The town itself had already been renamed Williamsburg.[5]

Not long after the burning of Jamestown's statehouse complex, another building, long since fallen into disuse, also collapsed in flames. Nathaniel Bacon's Curles Plantation had endured a generation of neglect and vandalism before tumbling in upon itself as flames consumed it. The remaining windowpanes melted or shattered, and the leaded latticework into which they had been set dropped out of their settings and curled into rolls of lumpy metal. The remains of the house remained undisturbed for nearly three centuries, buried in the rubble of Bacon's American plantation until they were excavated by archaeologists in the 1980s.[6]

The capital's move from Jamestown to Williamsburg and the final destruction of Bacon's home coincided with other transitions. With each passing year fewer people remained who had witnessed Bacon's Rebellion first hand. John Washington, Giles Brent, Robert Beverley, George Mason, Abraham Wood, Augustine Warner, and many others were already dead, having passed from the scene in the late 1670s and 1680s. John Coode died in 1699,

Excavations at Curles Plantation in the 1980s uncovered the ruins of Nathaniel Bacon's home, which fell into disuse after his death in October 1676 and then was consumed by fire around 1700. (Courtesy of the Anthropology Program, School of World Studies, Virginia Commonwealth University)

dismissed by Nicholson as "not fit for human much less Christian Society" but unscathed for his part in the rebellion. Isaac Allerton passed away in 1702, William Byrd in 1704, and Arthur Allen in 1709.[7]

To the delight of Bacon's heirs, entire peoples also passed from the scene as Nicholson and Andros presided over the dispossession of one Indian nation after another. The Appomattox asked permission to live among the English in 1691, giving up on owning their own lands except as private individuals under English law. Chickahominies, Nanzaticos—in fact, almost every nation—lost land through sales, often illegal, and through white settlers squatting on their lands. The Pamunkeys, still in possession of a substantial reservation in the immediate aftermath of Bacon's Rebellion, lost so much of their land to squatters and sales in the 1690s that not enough remained to support the population.[8]

Smallpox aided the colonists' efforts to dispossess their Indian neighbors. A major epidemic broke out in the winter of 1696, aided by unusually cold, snowy weather that forced people to crowd together indoors. Thousands, white and black, free and unfree, fell ill with the dread disease. There had been no recent smallpox epidemics in the region, so few people enjoyed any degree of resistance to the disease—least of all the neighbor Indians. By the time the epidemic had passed only four nations were left along the James River, ten nations on the entire Western Shore, and another nine on the Eastern Shore. The total Native population had plummeted to barely 1,400 people. "The Indians in Virginia," Andros concluded, "are so decreased as now hardly worth the name of Nations."[9]

Colonists especially appreciated Nicholson's uncompromising stance toward neighbor Indians. In 1695 Nicholson broke off diplomatic relations with Maryland's oldest allies, the Piscataways, henceforth treating them as subjects of the king rather than as an independent nation. He opened the Piscataways' territory to English settlement. By 1697 most Piscataways had taken up new quarters on the upper Potomac, safely above the English settlements. Nicholson gladly let them go. He "could have the Emperor of Piscattoway and his Indians knocked in the head," he commented, but it was easier to leave them to "be sick and starve in the mountains."

Giving up on Virginia and Maryland, the Piscataways looked instead to Pennsylvania. Many of the Susquehannocks had returned to their pre-1673 homeland on the lower Susquehanna River. Refugees from other nations, such as the Shawnees, were also gravitating to the Susquehanna, often under the protection of the Iroquois. In 1701 the Piscataways abandoned their long-term connection to Maryland in favor of a new alliance with Pennsylvania, the Iroquois, and the Susquehanna River nations, eventually establishing a town of their own there. Although individual people and families stayed behind along the Potomac, the independent Piscataway nation was no more.[10]

The Nanzaticos fared even worse than the Piscatways. English planters began nibbling away at their homeland along the Rappahannock River as early as the 1650s. By the 1670s many Nanzaticos had fallen into servitude, working alongside indentured servants and enslaved Africans on what had very recently been their own lands. During Bacon's Rebellion they hid in the woods and swamps, and when they emerged they found that even more of their lands had been appropriated. White squatters moved in on what was left, and their crops were repeatedly damaged by free-ranging English livestock.

By the spring of 1704 they had had enough. An English neighbor had torn down their fences and evicted them from their land. They complained to Nicholson but received no response. A second petition, asking the Council for relief from harassment by a local family named Rowley, also went nowhere. On August 30 a handful of Nanzatico men, painted for war, fell upon the Rowleys and killed the entire family. The county militia arrested every Nanzatico they could find—forty-nine of them—and stole or destroyed most of their possessions.

Five Nanzaticos confessed to the Rowley killings and were swiftly hanged as other neighbor Indians looked on. The remaining forty-four adults and children were sent to Williamsburg and locked up in the new jail that Nicholson had built. After considerable deliberation the Assembly sold thirteen Nanzatico children into servitude until they turned twenty-four; if the girls had children before their release, their infants, too, would be made servants for twenty-four years. The children were prohibited from visiting Indian towns for the rest of their lives. The remaining Nanzaticos—everyone over eleven—were "Transported beyond [the] Sea" to be sold into seven years of servitude in the West Indian sugar island of Antigua. None returned. If there were any survivors, they simply vanished into the population of enslaved Africans.[11]

Most new Indian slaves came to Virginia from points farther south, where warfare, slavery, epidemics, and rivalries between European powers were transforming the face of Indian country.

This instability ensured a steady flow of captives who could be sold into slavery within Virginia or into an even more horrific life laboring in the sugar plantations of the West Indies. The practice was so unexceptional that Indian slaves normally appeared in English records only in passing unless, as in the case of four Tuscaroras sold to the West Indies in 1690, their relatives threatened war against the English. Between the Virginia traders and the increasingly successful Carolina-based Indian traders, English goods had become plentiful among southern Indians—and Indian slaves were increasingly plentiful among the English.[12]

The accelerating changes left a trail of wreckage wherever Virginians, Carolinians, and other Europeans penetrated the backcountry. English traders introduced smallpox and other diseases, setting off epidemics that spread deep into the interior. Indian slave raids for English markets reached as far south and west as Florida and the Mississippi River. At a sober estimate 30,000–50,000 southern Indians were enslaved by the British between 1670 and 1715, with at least half of that growth coming after 1700. Entire peoples disappeared or were integrated into more successful nations, such as the Creeks, Catawbas, Cherokees, and Yamasees. Gaping holes in the map opened up as places once inhabited by numerous smaller nations became buffer zones between a smaller number of larger nations.

In the North, too, patterns of war, trade, and peace were changing at the turn of the century. Major treaties in 1701 between the Iroquois, French, and western Indian nations at Montréal and between the Iroquois and English at Albany freed Five Nations warriors to raid more frequently and deeply into the South while also constraining them, for the time being, from intruding too much into English settlements. Although the English and French would fight more wars, the two treaties of 1701 allowed the Iroquois to play the two European powers against one another, for the most part avoiding war with either the French or the English.[13]

The Indian slave trade, for all of its explosive growth, was soon dwarfed by the importation of enslaved Africans. Wealthy Virginia planters at mid-century had been early adopters, acquiring a disproportionate share of the few enslaved Africans available before the 1690s, but that meager supply had been insufficient to establish Africans as the colony's main source of labor. Changes in the Atlantic slave trade, however, made many more Africans available for purchase in the 1690s, with as many entering in the five years before 1700 as in the previous twenty years; thus the enslaved population increased twice as fast as the white population between 1680 and 1720.[14]

The shift from servants to slaves brought with it a fundamental reappraisal of Virginia's law, society, culture, and politics. One could clearly see this shift taking place in a wholesale overhaul of Virginia's laws ordered by the crown in 1698 and enacted by the Assembly in 1705. The centerpiece of this effort, the lengthy "Act concerning Servants and Slaves," radically simplified race relations by consistently placing white people on one side and everyone else on the other. "No negros, mulattos, or Indians" could own white servants. Free people (disproportionately white) were prohibited from dealing with servants and slaves (disproportionately nonwhite) without the master's permission. And legislators were at considerable pains to outlaw interracial sex and marriage, particularly involving white women. The previous law implicitly permitting Indian slavery was reaffirmed: "all servants imported and brought into this country, by sea or land, who were not christians in their native country . . . shall be accounted and be slaves." Further driving a wedge between white servants and nonwhite slaves were provisions sheltering servants from abuse by their masters—protections that were not available to slaves.

Two of the most important tools for separating whites from nonwhites were embedded within new laws that did not, on the surface, seem to have much to do with Indians or race. "An act declaring who shall not bear office in this country" attempted a legal definition of race in cases of mixed parentage, declaring that "the child of an Indian and the child, grand child, or great grand child, of a negro shall be deemed, accounted, held and taken to be a mulatto," and thus more likely to be enslaved. And perhaps most critically, buried deep within a law organizing the colony's General Court was a provision that "negroes, mulattoes and Indian servants" could not testify as witnesses "in any cases whatsoever." How, then, could Indian servants prove that they were being held beyond their terms? Without Indian testimony, what was to prevent masters from keeping Indian servants as slaves or taking their lands in legal actions?[15]

True to his aversion to public affairs, Thomas Mathew had retired from public office after returning from the dramatic 1676 session of the Assembly. No longer even a member of the county court, Mathew focused on his private life and business. By 1680 he had imported more than seventy-five servants and slaves into Virginia, including at least thirteen enslaved Africans. In retirement Mathew returned to his native London where, in 1705, the powerful secretary of state Robert Harley requested that he write an account of "The Beginning, Progress, and Conclusion of Bacon's Rebellion, 1675–1676."

Pleading that he was more comfortable with numbers than with words, and that in the thirty years since the rebellion many things "are laps'd out of mind, and others Imperfectly retained," Mathew pledged to stay narrowly on "the Track of barefac'd Truths." This proved impossible, for Mathew was fascinated by what he regarded as the larger, even cosmic dimensions of the rebellion. His "barefac'd truths," it turned out, included the comet and other "Ominous Presages" that foreshadowed the rebellion, the "Charme" by which Bacon "conjur'd" his initial followers into his circle, and the "Sorceries of the Indians" that caused a cloud to follow Bacon about during his summer of rebellion.

Mathew ended his story somewhat abruptly and prematurely, as if he no longer had the energy to set down the vivid details that marked the earlier portions of his account. Perhaps he really was too tired to go on: he died only a few months after finishing the tale. His account survived in manuscript for nearly a century, changing hands an untold number of times before an American diplomat purchased it in London and sent it to President Thomas Jefferson in 1803. It was published for the first time in a Virginia newspaper in 1804. By then even Mathew's children had long since passed from the scene.[16]

The first *published* historical account of Bacon's Rebellion appeared in the 1705 *History and Present State of Virginia* by Robert Beverley, Jr. The son of William Berkeley's lieutenant during the rebellion, the son-in-law of William Byrd, a Jamestown resident, and the brother of a provincial clerk, Beverley was uniquely positioned to tell the story.

Although he rejected Bacon's Rebellion as "illegitimate," Beverley offered a cool-headed analysis of the rebellion's causes. They amounted to four: a persistently weak tobacco economy, the confusion caused by giving large land grants to private individuals in northern Virginia (and the heavy taxes that had to be laid to pay for agents of the colony to live in London while lobbying for the repeal of those grants); the "heavy Restraints and Burdens" on trade (particularly the tax on tobacco and the exclusion of Dutch competitors from the market); and finally—especially—the "Disturbance given by the Indians." This last cause was critical, for the people, their "Minds already full of Discontent," could most easily express their frustrations by "vent[ing] all their Resentment against the poor Indians." At first the mob "flock'd together tumultuously, running in Troops from one Plantation to another without a Head," Beverly noted, but with Bacon to lead them they channeled their discontent into a rebellion.

Although Beverley devoted considerable space in his book to the languages, rituals, and customs of Virginia's Indians, he seemed only partly moved by his neighbors' struggles. "This harmless people," he wrote, were "happy, I think, in their simple State of Nature, and in their enjoyment of Plenty, without the Curse of Labour." Or so they had been before "the arrival of the Europeans, by whose means they seem to have lost their Felicity, as well as their Innocence." It was a remarkably bland way of describing a century of violence, some of the worst of which had occurred during Beverley's lifetime. "The Indians of Virginia are almost wasted," he wrote, but he failed to note that the pace of that wasting had accelerated during Bacon's Rebellion and its after-math, let alone that the Nanzaticos were being eliminated as a people and sold into slavery just as he was completing his *History*.

Beverley concluded with a list of Indian nations remaining in Virginia. On the Southern Piedmont, still largely outside the English settlements, the Nottoways still had a hundred "bow men" and the Meherrins forty. The Pamunkeys too had about forty warriors left, but they were in "decrease." Those were the fortunate nations. The Chickahominies, near Jamestown, were down to sixteen bowmen, and the Rappahannocks were "reduc'd to a few Families, and live scatter'd upon the English Seats." Nathaniel Bacon's very first victims, the Appomattox, were living in the pasture of Beverley's recently deceased father-in-law William Byrd, "not being above seven Families." It was the final appearance of the Appomattox people in the English records.[17]

Two years after the publication of the *History*, Beverley jotted down the tale of an Indian he had just interviewed. The man, as far as Beverley could make out, was a twenty-six-year-old named Lamhatty. At least that was what it sounded like to the English; when Beverley met Lamhatty no one had yet been found who understood the captive's language. Thus Beverley's account, written on one side of a single sheet of paper, had to be based on a combination of information from other planters who had already met Lamhatty, on Lamhatty's gestures, and, most unusually, on a map of the route by which Lamhatty arrived in Virginia.

That journey had begun at Lamhatty's Towasa town, far to the southwest on the Alabama River near the Gulf of Mexico. The

Tuscaroras, the Iroquoian people just south of Virginia, had during the "foregoing year . . . made war on the Towasas and destroyed 3 of theyr nations (the whole consisting of ten)." Then, "haveing disposed of theyr prisoners," they returned in the spring of 1707 and "swept away 4 nations more." It was this "second comeing" that ensnared Lamhatty. The Tuscaroras carried him northward and sold him to the Savannahs, still living along the Savannah River.

But the Savannahs were just then preparing to abandon their town. They had been relative newcomers to the South anyway, part of a large-scale scattering of groups from the Ohio Valley by Iroquois raiders during the 1660s and 1670s. By 1707 the chaos of the previous decades and the impact of smallpox, slave raids, and the arming of ever more southern nations had caught up with them. The Savannahs had decided to move to Pennsylvania to join the growing multiethnic consortium of Delawares, Susque-hannocks, Piscataways, and other nations.

Lamhatty came with them. Carried northward by a party of eleven Savannahs, he noted that they were hugging the foot of the north-running Appalachian ridges. After six weeks they pitched camp near the headwaters of the Rappahannock River. That was where he made his move, running away toward the English set-tlements. Naked and unarmed, he stumbled onto an English farm "in very bad weather in the Christmas holliday." At first the frightened English "Seized upon him violently and tyed him," even though he had made no attempt at resistance. But when Lamhatty wept and "shewed them how his hands were galled and swelled by being tyed" by his Savannah masters, they relented and "tyed the string onely by one arme" until they could bring him before a local militia commander, Lieutenant Colonel Walker. Walker, seeing that Lamhatty posed no threat, unbound him and kept him at his plantation.

When Beverley interviewed Lamhatty he was still "at liberty" and living in Walker's household. Afterward, though, it was discovered that some of Lamhatty's "Country folks" were already slaves on nearby plantations. This revelation changed Walker's attitude for the worse. From then on Lamhatty was "ill used," like a slave, and became "very melancholly." He fasted and wept for days at a time, and sometimes was witnessed "using [a] little Conjuration."

The following spring, when the weather grew warm, Lamhatty disappeared. Like so many other Indians during Bacon's Rebellion and its generation-long aftermath, he "went away" and "was never more heard of."[18]

Eastern North America, 1705

# AFTERWORD

THE FIRST WRITERS TO TELL THE STORY OF BACON'S REBELLION—
Robert Beverley prime among them—took Governor Berkeley's
side. A 1731 poem by Ebenezer Cooke called Bacon "A Man
respected by the Mob/As a fit Fool to do their Jobb," while William
Keith, in his 1738 *History of the British Plantations in America*, wondered why anyone would rebel "against so good a Governor." Bacon
was typically presented as "a hot-headed young gentleman."

The American Revolution turned this interpretive world upside
down. Citizens of the new nation could not help but notice, and did
not think it a coincidence, that Bacon's rebels had risen up against a
royal governor exactly 100 years before the signing of the Declaration of Independence. "Nathaniel Bacon will be no longer regarded
as a rebel, but as a patriot," noted one history in 1804. From then
until the 1950s Bacon's Rebellion was routinely presented as a pre-
cursor of the American Revolution, a premature revolt against British tyranny that represented only a temporary setback for the
unstoppable cause of American liberty. Bacon stood for "justice,
freedom, and humanity." He was "the author, and George Washington, the finisher," of America's revolutionary ideals.[1]

This viewpoint found its strongest expression in Thomas Wertenbaker's *Torchbearer of the Revolution: The Story of Bacon's Rebellion and Its Leader* (1940). Contrasting the reactionary forces led by Berkeley, the "archenemy of colonial democracy," and the freedom-loving planters led by Bacon, "the true seventeenth-century patriot, who gave his life in the cause of American liberty," Wertenbaker argued that Bacon's Rebellion was really about "whether the mass of people . . . were to control the government, or whether there was to be a degraded peasantry held under the heel of the mother country."[2]

But as modern historians have pointed out, Wertenbaker's account is simply incompatible with the evidence. Bacon himself indignantly denied having any democratic ("leveling") tendencies. His was a rebellion *for* Charles II, in the king's interests—or, at least, he recognized that he would lose his followers, and his head, if he did not appear to be on the king's side. It was the corrupt governor Berkeley and his followers who were the real traitors, Bacon argued. Moreover, the rise of the civil rights movement in the mid-twentieth century made it increasingly difficult to explain how the rebels' allegedly democratic, humane ideals fit with the racist principles that guided their behavior. "Should a democratic champion of the oppressed," asked one of Wertenbaker's critics, "limit his benevolence to whites only?" Small wonder, then, that a modern historian has called *Torchbearer of the Revolution* "one of the worst books on Virginia that a reputable scholarly historian ever published."[3]

Wilcomb Washburn, a pugnacious young graduate student in history in the 1950s, was especially perplexed by Wertenbaker's interpretation. While conducting research on another topic,

Washburn had stumbled upon a treasure trove of unexamined documents at the country estate of the man who had been England's secretary of state during Bacon's Rebellion. Using these materials Washburn wrote *The Governor and the Rebel: A History of Bacon's Rebellion in Virginia* (1957), in which he dismissed the notion of Bacon as a democratic reformer. The Baconites' "real grievance against Governor Berkeley," Washburn wrote, was that "he refused to authorize the slaughter and dispossession of the innocent as well as the 'guilty.'" Far from being an oppressed class, English folk along the Virginia frontier—rich and poor alike—raged against the governor who dared to restrain their racist, oppressive Indian policies.[4]

Washburn revealed a whole new way of understanding the rebellion. What, after all, was more central to American history than race, Indian dispossession, and slavery? Edmund S. Morgan's 1975 classic *American Slavery, American Freedom: The Ordeal of Colonial Virginia*, pressed that line of questioning much further. The central paradox in all of American history, he wrote, was that the American revolutionaries who spoke most movingly about liberty—men such as Patrick Henry, Thomas Jefferson, and James Madison—were disproportionately Virginia slaveowners. Bacon's Rebellion, Morgan argued, was the pivotal moment in a long process during which "slavery and freedom made their way to England's first American colony and grew there together, the one supporting the other." This was America's original sin, the equivalent of Adam and Eve plucking the forbidden fruit and causing no end of grief for their descendants.

There are, of course, other ways of interpreting Bacon's Rebellion. Some writers have focused closely on the inner workings of

Virginia, debating exactly where the divisions lay within colonial society on the eve of the rebellion. Others have returned to the question of what Bacon's Rebellion tells us about the place of America within the British Empire. For Stephen Saunders Webb, for instance, Bacon's Rebellion was nothing less than an attempted revolution. It frightened Charles II into imposing a "new-model imperial government" that brushed aside both the rebels' complaints *and* the system of semi-independent colonial government that had developed under Berkeley's decades-long governorship. The result, as the title of Webb's 1984 book announced, was "The End of American Independence."[5]

*Torchbearer of the Revolution; American Slavery, American Freedom; 1676: The End of American Independence*: the memorable titles ringingly declare each author's central theme. What, then, is *Tales from a Revolution* getting at? And what are the "transformations" hinted at in the subtitle of this book?

It is, to begin with, a tale—a story, a narrative, a yarn. Such an approach is more controversial than one might imagine, because historians have a complicated relationship with narrative. The discipline boasts a long tradition of narrative writing, of course, and a casual examination of most any bookstore's shelves will reveal that narrative history is alive and well. Yet historians are also acutely aware of narrative's limits. The point of history is to explore *why* things happened as they did, and narrative can actually make it harder for writers and readers to think clearly about the "why" question.

Narrative is sneaky. Its writers find it all too easy to smuggle into a story ideas and assertions that would not hold up if they were stated explicitly and accompanied by a careful analysis of the evidence. The fragmentary nature of the evidence often forces a historian to go out on a limb and speculate a little, but in a narrative there is little room for the writer to discuss such issues. Take, for example, the cause of Bacon's death. Diagnosing a patient who has been dead for several centuries is, to put it mildly, an inexact science. My narrative suggests that typhus killed Bacon, and I think that's right—or at least that the diagnosis of typhus is most consistent with the few fragmentary bits of information provided by people who weren't actually there when he died. Of course, either the evidence or my interpretation of it may be flawed. Yet to pause in the middle of the story to weigh all the relevant considerations in this diagnosis would have been awkward. Too many such interruptions, and soon the story—this "tale"—would cease to be a story at all.

Narrative can also oversimplify complex situations. It may seem as if there are already too many different characters in this story. The cast of Indian nations alone is extensive. And yet I've left out entire nations where it was possible to use one group to communicate the same essential point. There were at least six nations, for example, involved in the Occaneechees' attack against the Susquehannocks, but I mentioned only two. Similarly, I might have done more to explore the geography of the rebellion had such an analysis lent itself better to the narrative mode. Experts might also be surprised at how I've pushed Lady Frances Berkeley and the customs collector Giles Bland to the margins; in another story, focusing on different dimensions of the rebellion, they would be major characters. A related problem with narrative is that the urge to define complex situations in terms of one-on-one struggles between two individuals is almost irresistible. Indeed, some historians have been so captivated by the struggle between the governor and the rebel that they have failed to notice that their deaths, so conveniently close in time, did not resolve the issues that their followers were fighting over (let alone that Indians were involved in the story for reasons of their own, which also did not end with the deaths of the two men).

Narrative history has its limitations, then. Does it have virtues? After writing this story, I am more than ever convinced that it does. I set out to integrate historians' best insights into Bacon's Rebellion within an engaging narrative, allowing those insights to emerge from the story ("show, don't tell," is a common writer's mantra). My starting point was not the scholarly imperative to develop a thesis (although I hoped to emerge with one after having told the story) but rather something akin to the novelist's imperative to develop a plot. As I had hoped, a narrative approach exposed dimensions of the rebellion that other historians had missed or only glanced at in passing. In other words, I learned things that might have escaped my attention had I written a different kind of book.

Novelists who set out to show rather than tell sometimes make use of what literary critics refer to as an "unreliable narrator," a character whose point of view is a little off, even delusional. As the writer David Lodge explains, that is the reason for letting an unreliable narrator speak: "to reveal in an interesting way the gap between appearance and reality, and to show how human beings distort or conceal the latter." Once readers notice that the narrator's version of events cannot be fully trusted, they are forced to think for themselves—to develop their own opinions about what really happened, and why.[6]

There was no shortage of unreliable narrators among the witnesses to Bacon's Rebellion. They told wild, irrational tales, full of paranoia, supernatural forces, superheated rhetoric, and outright misinformation. Are we really to believe Sarah Grendon, William Byrd's aunt, when she claims that Governor Berkeley would come into people's homes and confiscate their bedding to make up any shortfall in tax revenues? Did Indian "*Pawawing*" cause a rain cloud to follow Bacon's volunteers wherever they went, and drought wherever they were not? Can we accept at face value the claim that Lord Baltimore was an evil genius whose every move was part of an intricate plan to "intangle our innocent posterity under that tyranicall yoake of papacy?" Did 10,000 Iroquois warriors—a figure that exceeded the total population of the Five Nations, let alone its warriors—actually assemble on the upper Potomac in the spring of 1689 and build a fort there before anyone noticed them? Of course not.

Yet unreliable narrators such as Nathaniel Bacon, Sarah Grendon, Thomas Mathew, and the author of the "Complaint from Heaven" reveal much about the passions that drove events in the late seventeenth century. To a remarkable extent, the events of the rebellion were driven by gossip, rumor, misinformation, and contending stories. Sometimes there was nothing else to go on. People made their choices in the absence of information, operating within what is often called the "fog of war"—which, as the great Prussian military theorist Carl von Clausewitz described it, "gives to things exaggerated dimensions and an unnatural appearance."[7]

Historians have done an admirable job of reconstructing the objective reasons for the discontent within Virginia and Maryland during these decades. But to understand why discontent turned into rebellion, we need to appreciate the colonists' fear, anger, and suspicious-mindedness; their paranoia and susceptibility to conspiracy theories; their vengefulness and malice; and their willingness to resort to violence, savagery, oppression, and cruelty when they felt threatened by Indians, governors, "Papists," or anyone else outside their tribe. We need to appreciate that they believed in magic, Satan, and God, and that in their eyes supernatural beings played a decisive role in human affairs.

A narrative doesn't simply arrange events chronologically. In most cases it opens, as does this book, with a chapter introducing the characters, their conflicts, and their dilemmas. The conflicts and dilemmas are the most important part, because those are the sources of narrative tension that will keep the story moving right through to the end. The rising action follows this introduction, often reaching a false climax—in the case of this tale, with the deaths of the governor and the rebel in Chapter 7. At such points (to quote one novelist) the story "gathers itself . . . changes strategy, and freshens."[8] The rising action, thus reset, then peaks at the tale's 90-percent mark (here, with the climactic events of the Glorious Revolution). The denouement ushers the characters offstage at what seems like a reasonable stopping point, though inevitably loose ends remain.

Constructing a story in this fashion may slant the narrative in certain directions, but doing so does not necessarily make it any less true. In fact, ordering the narrative in this way can reveal things that would have otherwise gone unnoticed. The key lies in the focus on unresolved tensions. Real life is full of such dilemmas: who, if anyone, to marry; whether to embark on a life of adventure or stay close to one's roots; when to break with custom and act according to conscience and when to conform to society's traditional judgment. We face collective dilemmas as well, most often forcing us to choose what kind of people we (insert the name of your group here) want to be. Working through these decisions is an unavoidable part of the human condition. Films, novels, and other stories, with their central device of creating and resolving dramatic tension, are excellent vehicles for thinking about how the world really works and thus about how we might work through our own dilemmas.

Similarly, looking for the sources of dramatic tension in Bacon's Rebellion is a good way of exploring how the world worked at a pivotal moment in American history. As I see it, two related dilemmas lay at the heart of the conflicts among Indians and colonists. The colonists' dilemma was how to relieve the pressures on "the people" without either dismantling the existing social and political structure or dispensing with "English liberties." The Indians' dilemma was how to survive the onslaught of English planters and slave traders without plunging into a war that might destroy them.

These dilemmas could not be resolved through the deaths of the governor and the rebel. Far from it. The real conflicts underlying Bacon's Rebellion took decades to settle, and the resolutions to these conflicts transformed early America. The changes involved were vast: they extended through much of eastern America, across the Atlantic Ocean, and into the most profound and intimate aspects of human existence.

The dilemmas of both Indians and colonists resolved themselves through the transformation of Native American life in eastern North America, and particularly in the Southeast. The primary engine of this transformation was the expansion of the European economy into Indian country. The volume of trade between southern Indians and colonists mushroomed in the late seventeenth century, providing the newcomers with furs, pelts, and Indian slaves captured in war, in exchange for cloth, metal tools, and other manufactured goods.

These European goods included guns, which helped those Indians with the best trading connections to attack less heavily armed nations and to take still more captives to be sold into slavery—thus further strengthening their connections with the colonists. Taking captives had long been an important social and cultural practice for Native Americans. Now it became central to the economies and diplomatic strategies of the most successful slaving nations. Trading alliances such as those connecting the Occaneechees and Westos to Virginia ensured a steady inflow of guns, ammunition, and wealth, which strengthened those nations in dangerous times.

War, combined with diseases introduced through the trade with Europeans, sent Native populations spiraling downward, making it ever more difficult for communities to defend against slavers and encroaching English farmers. The result was a reshuffling of peoples throughout the eastern woodlands, with Native communities constantly migrating to new locations that were less directly in harm's way, merging with other communities to form larger groupings, and gradually consolidating into a smaller number of distinct nations. As one nation after another disappeared from the map, the captives feeding the growing Indian slave trade had to be drawn from an ever-shrinking pool. If the cycle continued, everyone was bound in the end to become victims of the slave trade.

By 1715, as one writer has noted, virtually every Indian community in the South was caught in a web "of debt, slaving, militarization, and warfare" from which they could not escape, even though the system was "crumbling under its own brutal weight." Some tried: the powerful Tuscarora nation of North Carolina launched a war against the colonists in 1711, and the Yamasee War of 1715 spread from Carolina's Atlantic coast to the Mississippi River. In each case the offensive failed, suppressed by a combination of provincial troops and their allies among other Indian nations. The surviving Tuscaroras and Yamasees were enslaved or migrated away from their Carolina homes, the Tuscaroras going north to become the sixth nation of the Iroquois League and the Yamasees taking refuge in Spanish Florida. After these two wars the Indian slave trade began a long decline. Deerskins replaced people as the primary object of intercultural trade, and the African slave trade increasingly supplied the colonial labor market.[9]

Virginia's and Maryland's "neighbor Indians," of course, were also swept up in the transformation of Indian country. The removal of Berkeley and Baltimore from power left the Indian allies of these men more vulnerable than ever to slavers and encroaching English planters. No longer much needed as military allies or trading partners, they had little to offer colonists except their bodies and their lands. Dispossessed and marginalized, neighbor Indians sometimes migrated and merged with a larger, more powerful Indian nation, as the Susquehannocks and Piscataways did when they moved north under Iroquois protection. Those who remained in their homelands were demoted from nations to racial minorities, each group struggling even to survive as a community and a culture. Many fell into servitude or slavery on English plantations. Almost always, in the end, they lost their lands to English farmers.

In short, the Baconites won the battle over how best to deal with Native Americans. From their perspective the shift in strategy worked spectacularly well. In 1675 Indians still controlled affairs outside a narrow band of European settlements along the coast, but by the early eighteenth century colonists had gained the upper hand. To be sure, decades remained before all of the Native peoples east of the Mississippi had suffered the fate of the Pamunkeys, Occaneechees, and Piscataways, but Nathaniel Bacon's domineering, uncompromising, and indiscriminate approach to Indian affairs, rather than Berkeley's web of trade and alliances, became Virginia's default mode. Eventually it would become the default mode in other colonies and states, and even for the United States government itself.

The intra-Indian wars and Indian slave trade worked profoundly to the colonists' benefit. The slave trade subsidized the English economy through theft, because Indian slaves brought into the trade were stolen, not purchased. For individual planters, the addition of even one or two Indian laborers made a tremendous difference in an era when there were neither enough white indentured servants nor enslaved Africans to supply the colonies' needs. Then too, the shift in the balance of power from Indians to colonists made the frontiers safer places for the English to live, and the migration or dispossession of neighbor Indians cleared the way for more colonists and their slaves to spread over the countryside.

The increasingly uncompromising attitude of colonial governments toward Indians also helped to unify colonists. Debates over
Indian policy, once deeply divisive, almost disappeared from
public life. Between 1677 and 1687 Virginia's governors concluded
a handful of essential treaties, but after 1687 treaty negotiations
were rare. Virginia did not bother to renew its peace with the Iroquois until 1722. Virginia's and Maryland's governors did little or
nothing to restrain colonists from abusing Virginia's neighbor
Indians or from encouraging the spiraling cycle of wars and
slaving that fed the Virginia traders' business with the southern
nations. "A Governour of Virginia," explained one of Berkeley's
successors, "has to steer between Scylla and Charybdis, either an
Indian or a civil war, for the famous insurrection in this colony
called Bacon's Rebellion, was occasioned purely by the Governour
and Council refusing to let the people go out against the Indians."[10]

The Glorious Revolution marked a major turning point, a climax
in which the colonists found a resolution to the dilemmas
expressed in Bacon's Rebellion. It swept away Maryland's proprietary government, which had continued to approach Indian affairs
much as Berkeley had, and brought in Francis Nicholson as the
long-term governor of Virginia (1690–1692 and 1698–1704) and
Maryland (1694–1698). Under Nicholson the assaults against the
neighbor Indians accelerated, resulting in the scattering of the Piscataways and Nanzaticos and in the more quiet erosion of the land
base and populations of the Pamunkeys and other peoples. No one
could accuse Nicholson, or any other governor after 1689, of favoring his "protected and Darling Indians," as Bacon had accused
Berkeley of doing.

Virginians and Marylanders considered themselves to be subjects of the English king and as living on British soil. Though provincials, they closely participated in their nation's civic life. For them, Bacon's Rebellion was of a piece with the other major political stories of the 1670s: the rising power of France under the absolutist Sun King, Louis XIV; the increasing suspicion that Charles II was a secret Catholic; the certainty, after 1673, that Charles's brother and heir to the throne, James Duke of York, was a "papist"; the policy of greater religious toleration promoted by both Charles and James, which seemed like a trick to allow Catholicism to reconquer Protestant England; the Popish Plot of 1678–1681; and, in the end, the birth of James II's son, who (because he was a boy) would leapfrog over James's Protestant daughters Mary and Anne as heir to the crown—a *Catholic* heir.

In America, these frightening developments echoed in local conditions. Louis XIV oversaw a rapid expansion in the size and influence of New France, expanding the Canadian province into the Great Lakes and beyond until it encircled the British colonies by meeting up on the Mississippi River with French Louisiana. The expansion of New France was accomplished less through the conquest and repeopling of Native lands than through Indian trade and diplomacy, often conducted with the help of Catholic missionaries among the Indians. To many English colonists these events confirmed their worst fears. They had "known," already, that all Indians were on the same side, threatening a general combination against the English. Now the French, aided by Catholic missionaries (*Satan's* missionaries, they believed), were organizing the Indians into a vast plot reaching far beyond even Nathaniel Bacon's dire imaginings. Thus even as Bacon's Rebellion was being suppressed,

This playing card, printed in 1644, belonged to the future Louis XIV of France. The pleasant country inhabited by the English colonists, the card explains, was close to New France. Virginians were uncomfortably aware of that fact. (Courtesy of the Virginia Historical Society)

the stakes involved appeared to have grown, at least to the author of the "Complaint from Heaven" and other unrepentant Baconites.

The Glorious Revolution in England and America neatly resolved this tension by eliminating Catholics from positions of power. Before that upheaval, every move by the king, his appointed officials, and Baltimore's government had been scrutinized, lest it open the way to "popery." But with James II and the Calvert family set aside and Catholics barred from political life, conspiracy theories and anti-Catholic politics lost their traction.

After the Glorious Revolution, anti-Catholicism unified rather than divided colonists and other Englishmen. The popish menace within England had been suppressed and England's Protestantism was celebrated as a contrast to the despotism of Catholic monarchies, especially that of France's Louis XIV. If left unchecked France would extend its iron rule over more and more people, including, perhaps, England and its colonies. This new phase of the long war against "popery" and "french Despotick Rule" necessitated a more powerful, centralized imperial government to coordinate the struggle. William took England into battle against France in 1689, and the military buildup continued even after peace was made in 1697. The Board of Trade was established in 1696 to coordinate imperial affairs, and a series of other measures knit the empire into a closer economic union through a system of protective convoys and commercial regulation.

The invention of Britain as a nation was, as historian Linda Colley writes, "forged above all by war" against the French in 1689–1697, in 1702–1714, 1744–1748, 1754–1763, and beyond. "They [British citizens] defined themselves as Protestants struggling for survival against the world's foremost Catholic power. . . . They came to define themselves as a single people not because of any political or cultural consensus at home, but rather in reaction to the Other beyond their shores." Britain became the rational, commercial, virtuous, and free opposition to the "superstitious, militarist, decadent and unfree" nation across the Channel.[11]

The invention of the British nation in the decades following 1689 very much included Virginia and Maryland. Religion, commerce, and imperial governance, all mobilized against French Catholic tyranny, bound colonists together as Britons in a way that they had not been in 1676. A tightly integrated system of naval patrols, customs collectors, shipping convoys, and seasonal shipping embargos effectively shored up tobacco prices, helped the planter elite to consolidate their power within the colony, and harnessed Virginia and Maryland more fully to the needs of the growing British empire.

Nicholson's designs for the new capital cities of Williamsburg and Annapolis gave material expression to this trend, while within courtrooms and legislative chambers provincial authorities adhered more closely with each passing year to English common law and parliamentary procedure. In such settings they also celebrated the "rights of Englishmen" and "British liberties" that distinguished them from the French and other benighted Catholic nations. Planters who could afford to do so also strove to act more like the English provincial gentry. Mansions in the new Georgian style replaced makeshift wooden structures, and formal English gardens were added to the functional farmyards of the seventeenth century. Elite planters' children were increasingly educated by English tutors or even sent to England for schooling. The more refined English manners, such as using a handkerchief or a fork or saying "please" and "thank you," were quickly taken up by leading planters. Like the English gentry, they also embraced high standards of hospitality and generosity toward visitors, even strangers, and in return expected greater deference from their less successful neighbors.

But how to secure that deference? Herein lay a problem. Not all of the tensions within colonial society could be relieved by the expulsion of James II and Lord Baltimore, nor by any campaign for British unity. The "Poore Endebted Discontented and Armed" settlers who had so worried Governor Berkeley still found themselves squeezed by low tobacco prices, labor shortages, and high taxes. The decline in white indentured servitude, and thus of poor freedmen, helped to relieve some of the pressure by making it possible for a greater proportion of white men to establish independent households. So too did the increasing number of white women, because marrying and raising a family were keys to successful manhood in the planters' conception of the world.

Yet wealthy planters understood that their position remained precarious. They were anxious to improve the colony's economy, prevent another revolt by frustrated small to middling planters (let alone slaves and servants), and smooth over differences among the gentry that might threaten their success as a class. Even King William and his officials felt somewhat vulnerable, for the crown's substantial tax revenues from tobacco depended upon a healthy economy and political stability.

Race supplied the key to resolving these conflicts. Simply put, ordinary planters agreed to accept the rule of their elite superiors, while the gentry agreed to treat common planters and white servants more respectfully. And together, both sorts agreed to share the benefits of white supremacy. As Edmund S. Morgan put it, Bacon's Rebellion taught that "resentment of an alien race might be more powerful than the resentment of an upper class." Thus the codification of Virginia law culminating in 1705 drew a stark line between whites and everyone else, making it possible for those on the right side of that line to enjoy greater liberty and equality while also benefiting from the fruits of slavery.

Indeed, whites enjoyed greater liberty precisely *because* Indians and Africans enjoyed less of it. As one historian has noted, "liberty" was not a universal ideal in eighteenth-century America but rather "a privileged status that almost always depended upon the power to subordinate someone else." "Virginia's ruling class,"

Morgan observes, "proclaimed that all white men were superior to black." They backed it up by offering their "social (but white) inferiors" better opportunities as freedmen, including grants of land at the end of their terms of servitude, lower taxes, and more political power. Conveniently, there were fewer ex-servants to provide for, since the supply of white indentured servants was shrinking and the supply of slaves expanding. Slaves, of course, never had to be freed and did not have to be extended the rights and privileges of Englishmen.[12]

The implications of this new social order penetrated into almost every part of life. Racial slavery and white populism—white tribalism, one might say—forced Indians and Africans to shoulder the burden of resolving the tensions and divisions within colonial society. Now, a slave's every gesture and word was examined by whites for signs that racial discipline was being observed. As the slave population increased, even the poorest, unhappiest white Virginians were lifted further from the bottom of society. White men enjoyed a secure place in an all-white political culture revolving around militia musters, county court sessions, gambling, horse racing, athletic competitions, tavern life, and competitive elections in which gentry candidates were forced to appeal to their white inferiors for votes. All white men were at least "potential patriarchs."

This naturally had implications for women. White women lost political influence as men came to more fully dominate public life, but they gained status in other ways. Whereas formerly a white woman could be called anything from a "nasty wench" to a gentlewoman, with the rise of racial slavery "wench" came to be used almost exclusively to describe slave women. White women, it was assumed, were inherently virtuous. Black women became not only laborers for their masters, but also fair game—"wenches"—available for white men's sexual advances.[13]

The formula hit upon in the wake of Bacon's Rebellion worked well for white Virginians. By the eve of the American Revolution theirs was the most populous, wealthy, and influential colony in mainland British America. When its fortunes declined after the Revolution, thousands of migrants streamed westward through the gaps in the Appalachians to establish new communities modeled after the old, making Virginian ways a large part of the DNA of American life in general. Bacon's Rebellion was a critical element in the creation of the Old South, and thus an important passage in the story of race, slavery, freedom, and western expansion in American history.

What difference did Nathaniel Bacon make? As an individual, did he really alter the course of events? Or was he buffeted about by impersonal forces that no one person created or controlled, such as changes in tobacco prices or the supply of English indentured servants and African slaves?

This is one small variation of a universal question at the heart of the human condition. To what extent do you or I control our own lives? And to the extent that we do not, who or what *does* determine our fates? Perhaps the story I've told gives some sense of what even the most powerful of men were up against—the difficulties they faced in controlling events, and the deeper, less visible, and uncontrollable forces at work in the era of Bacon's Rebellion.

Yet narrative keeps pulling us back toward the personal, "what if" questions that keep open the possibility that a single individual can alter history in significant ways. What if Bacon had died young or Berkeley had not lived to a ripe old age? What if either man had migrated to a different place? (Young William Berkeley nearly accepted a diplomatic post in Istanbul before changing his mind and coming to Virginia in 1642.) What if Berkeley had abandoned his forts, Indian diplomacy, and focus on the Susquehannock enemy, instead taking the more popular and less expensive path by allowing volunteers to attack Indians—any Indians—at will? What if Posseclay had anticipated Bacon's assault on the Occaneechee town and simply locked him out, leaving the exhausted volunteers on the wrong side of the Roanoke River with little to eat and only a vague idea of where the Susquehannocks might be found? What if Berkeley had acted less leniently toward Bacon at the outset, or Baltimore had hanged Josias Fendall in 1660 or 1681? What if James II had not fathered a new, Catholic heir in 1688? Were the deeper forces at work in Bacon's Rebellion and its aftermath so powerful, the tensions within and between Indian and colonial societies so great, that even in the absence of Bacon another leader would have stepped forward to lead "Byrd's Rebellion" or "Brent's Rebellion"?

There is, of course, no definitive answer to such questions, let alone a way to resolve the eternal tension between fate and free will. But narrative, at least, refuses to let go these fundamental debates. It also keeps reminding us how big events are intertwined with intimate relationships: Bacon's cousinship with Lady Frances Berkeley, Coode's friendship with Fendall, Cockacoeske's neighborly (if not terribly cordial) relations with nearby English planters, a poor planter's doomed courtship of a potential wife, a slave woman's demeanor toward the plantation mistress, Lamhatty's deteriorating relationship with Colonel Walker. Indeed, the trans-formations wrought during and after Bacon's Rebellion only matter, in the end, because they made such a powerful difference in individual lives and relationships.

It was in those relationships, too, that one might find the most enduring legacies of Bacon's Rebellion, where we might see the uniqueness of that distant historical time shading into the more recognizable terrain of the human condition. The events of this difficult era created a mood, a psychology, that we might easily recognize today. Perhaps in any age fear gives birth to violence and oppression, and expresses itself through rumor, conspiracy theories, and tribalism. Such theories, no matter how tenuous their original connection to reality, can, by some mysterious, almost magical process, create a new reality in which even the greatest absurdities—such as eradicating Indians to make room for more slaves—come to be considered such good ideas that they hardly need be questioned.

# Abbreviations

| | |
|---|---|
| *Arch. Md.* | William Hand Browne et al., eds., *Archives of Maryland*, 72 vols. (Baltimore: Maryland Historical Society, 1883–1972) |
| *DRCHSNY* | E. B. O'Callaghan and B. Fernow, eds., *Documents Relative to the Colonial History of the State of New York*, 15 vols. (Albany: Weed, Parsons, 1856–1887) |
| *DVB* | *Dictionary of Virginia Biography* |
| *Executive Journals* | H. R. McIlwaine, ed., *Executive Journals of the Council of Colonial Virginia,* vol. 1 (Richmond: Virginia State Library, 1925) |
| Hening, *Statutes* | Wm. Hening, ed., *The Statutes at Large; Being a Collection of all the Laws of Virginia from the First Session of the Legislature in the Year 1619* (New York: R. & W. & G. Bartow, 1819–1823) |
| *MdHM* | *Maryland Historical Magazine* |
| *PWB* | Warren Billings, ed., *The Papers of Sir William Berkeley, 1605–1677* (Richmond: Library of Virginia, 2007) |

| VCRP | Virginia Colonial Records Project, Virginia Historical Society (microfilm) |
| VHS | Virginia Historical Society |
| VMHB | *Virginia Magazine of History and Biography* |
| WMQ | *William and Mary Quarterly* |

# Notes

## Chapter 1

1. Charles Andrews, ed., *Narratives of the Insurrections, 1675–1690* (New York: Charles Scribner's Sons, 1915), 15–16.

2. "Notes and Queries," *VMHB* 1 (1893), 201–2; "Virginia Gleanings in England," *VMHB* 15 (1907), 57.

3. Michael Oberg, ed., *Samuel Wiseman's Book of Record: The Official Account of Bacon's Rebellion in Virginia, 1676–1677* (Lanham, MD: Lexington Books, 2005), 142–43. On the Doegs, see James Rice, *Nature and History in the Potomac Country: From Hunter-Gatherers to the Age of Jefferson* (Baltimore: Johns Hopkins University Press, 2009), 137–38.

4. Andrews, *Narratives*, 16–17.

5. Andrews, *Narratives*, 16–17; "Private Baptism of Children," in *The Book of Common Prayer, and Administration of the Sacraments* (1662).

6. *Arch. Md.* 23: 188; Warren Billings, ed., *The Papers of Sir William Berkeley, 1605–1677* (Richmond: Library of Virginia, 2007), 507; Rice, *Nature and History*, 145–47.

7. Warren Billings, *Sir William Berkeley and the Forging of Colonial Virginia* (Baton Rouge: Louisiana State University Press, 2004); Christopher Everett, "'They Shalbe Slaves for Their Lives': Indian Slavery in Colonial Virginia," in Allan Gallay, ed., *Indian Slavery in Colonial America* (Lincoln: University of Nebraska Press, 2009), 67–108; Helen Rountree, *Pocahontas's People: The Powhatan Indians of Virginia through Four Centuries* (Norman: University of Oklahoma Press, 1990).

8. Kathleen Brown, *Good Wives, Nasty Wenches, and Anxious Patri-archs: Gender, Race, and Power in Colonial Virginia* (Chapel Hill: University of North Carolina Press, 1996), ch. 5; John Coombs, "Beyond the Origins Debate: Rethinking the Rise of Virginia Slavery," in Douglas Bradburn and John C. Coombs, eds., *Early Modern Virginia: Reconsidering the Old Domin-ion* (Charlottesville: University of Virginia Press, 2011), 240–78; Lorena Walsh, *Motives of Honor, Pleasure, and Profit: Plantation Management in the Colonial Chesapeake, 1607–1763* (Chapel Hill: University of North Carolina Press, 2010), chs. 2–3; Brent Tarter, "Bacon's Rebellion, the Grievances of the People, and the Political Culture of Seventeenth-Century Virginia," *VMHB* 119 (2011), 16.

9. *PWB*, 321–22, 423, 507, 537.

10. John Krugler, *English and Catholic: The Lords Baltimore in the Seven-teenth Century* (Baltimore: Johns Hopkins University Press, 2004), 202–21.

11. H. R. McIlwaine, *Journals of the House of Burgesses of Virginia, 1659/60–1693* (Richmond: Colonial Press, 1915), 41; *PWB*, 485–86; *Arch. Md.* 15: 47–49.

12. *Arch. Md.* 2: 474–83; Andrews, *Narratives*, 19, 47–49; Lyon Tyler, "Col. John Washington: Further Details of His Life from the Records of Westmoreland Co., Virginia," *WMQ* 2 (1893), 38–42; Alice Ferguson, "The Susquehannock Fort on Piscataway Creek," *MdHM* 36 (1941), 1–9.

13. Everett, "'They Shalbe Slaves'"; April Hatfield, *Atlantic Virginia: Intercolonial Relations in the Seventeenth Century* (Philadelphia: University of Pennsylvania Press, 2004), 24–32; Martin Quitt, "William Byrd," *Dictio-nary of Virginia Biography*, Vol. 1 (Richmond: Library of Virginia, 1998), 463–66.

14. Robert Gunther, ed. *Further Correspondence of John Ray* (London, 1928), 32–35; Testament of Sir Edward Duke, Mss20855a1 o.s., VHS; *PWB*, 486–87, 530; Brent Tarter, "Nathaniel Bacon," *DVB* 1: 271–72.

## Chapter 2

1. "Bacon's Rebellion," *VMHB* 1 (1893), 180; Michael Oberg, ed., *Samuel Wiseman's Book of Record: The Official Account of Bacon's Rebellion in Vir-ginia, 1676–1677* (Lanham, MD: Lexington Books, 2005), 146.

2. Charles Andrews, ed., *Narratives of the Insurrections, 1675–1690* (New York: Charles Scribner's Sons, 1915), 20; Oberg, *Samuel Wiseman's Book of Record*, 144; *PWB*, 499, 509.

3. "Account of the estate of Nathaniel Bacon, Jr.," C.O.5/1371, Pt. II, 227–30, VCRP Reel 32 (the existence of the sheepfold, pastures, barn, and springhouse are inferred from the presence of related items in this inventory of Bacon's possessions); L. Daniel Mouer, "In the Realm of 'The Rebel': The Archaeology of Nathaniel Bacon's Brick House at Curles Plantation," *Henrico County Historical Society Magazine* 12 (1988), 3–20; *WMQ* 9 (1901), 4, 7, 10; Andrews, *Narratives*, 49–50; *PWB*, 498.

4. Oberg, *Samuel Wiseman's Book of Record*, 144; Francis Moryson to William Jones, October 1676, C.O.5/1371, Pt. I, VCRP reel 32.

5. *PWB*, 497–98, 504–9; Andrews, *Narratives*, 20–21; Oberg, *Samuel Wiseman's Book of Record*, 144–45; *WMQ* 9 (1900), 10.

6. William Kelso, *Jamestown: The Buried Truth* (Charlottesville: University of Virginia Press, 2006), 204–14; Warren Billings, *A Little Parliament: The Virginia General Assembly in the Seventeenth Century* (Richmond: Library of Virginia, 2004), ch. 10.

7. William Hening, ed., *The Statutes at Large*, vol. 2 (New York: R. & W. & G. Bartow, 1823), 326–36.

8. Andrews, *Narratives*, 50–51; *PWB*, 497–98, 535; Oberg, *Samuel Wiseman's Book of Record*, 145.

9. *PWB*, 536–37; Oberg, *Samuel Wiseman's Book of Record*, 145–47; Andrews, *Narratives*, 52–53; "Proclamations of Nathaniel Bacon," *VMHB* 1 (1893), 56–57; *WMQ* 9 (1900), 4, 6–7.

10. Oberg, *Samuel Wiseman's Book of Record*, 146–47.

## Chapter 3

1. Francis Jennings, *The Ambiguous Iroquois Empire: The Covenant Chain Confederation of Indian Tribes with English Colonies from Its Beginnings to the Lancaster Treaty of 1744* (New York: Norton, 1984), 149; William Sherwood, "Virginia's Deploured Condition," in *Collections of the Massachusetts Historical Society, Fourth Series*, Vol. 9 (1871), 167; *PWB*, 509; "Bacon's Rebellion," *VMHB* 1 (1893), 180. Posseclay is identified in some sources as "Persicles."

2. *PWB*, 517–21, 527–31; Wilcomb Washburn, *The Governor and the Rebel: A History of Bacon's Rebellion in Virginia* (New York: Norton, 1957), 189–90, n. 84; Charles Andrews, ed., *Narratives of the Insurrections, 1675–1690* (New York: Charles Scribner's Sons, 1915), 148; "Bacon's Rebellion," 180; Sherwood, "Deploured," 166–67.

3. Warren Billings, *The Old Dominion in the Seventeenth Century: A Documentary History of Virginia, 1606–1700*, rev. ed. (Chapel Hill: University of North Carolina Press, 2007), 330–33; "Bacon's Rebellion," 181–82; Sherwood, "Deploured," 166–69; *WMQ* 9 (1900), 7; Andrews, *Narratives*, 21; *PWB*, 523; *The Prose Works of William Byrd of Westover: Narratives of a Colonial Virginian*, ed. Louis B. Wright (Cambridge, MA: Harvard University Press, 1966), 384–87; "Occaneechee Island," *WMQ* 11 (1902), 121–22.

4. *PWB*, 522–23, 537.

5. *WMQ* 9 (1900), 8; "Bacon's Rebellion," 182; Sherwood, "Deploured," 169–70; Thomas Wertenbaker, *Torchbearer of the Revolution: The Story of Bacon's Rebellion and Its Leader* (Princeton, NJ: Princeton University Press, 1940), 54–55.

6. *PWB*, 523–26.

7. "Bacon's Rebellion," 180, 182; Billings, *The Old Dominion*, 333; *PWB*, 524.

## Chapter 4

1. Kenneth Scott and Kenn Stryker-Rodda, eds., *New York Historical Manuscripts: Dutch*, Vols. 20–21, trans. by Arnold J. F. Van Laer (Baltimore), 104 (quotation); *DRCHSNY* 1: 89, 13: 497–98 (quotations); Edwin Burrows and Mike Wallace, *Gotham: A History of New York City to 1898* (New York: Oxford University Press, 1999), 35–37, 65, 85–87. On treaty protocol, see Daniel Richter, *Facing East from Indian Country* (Cambridge, MA: Harvard University Press, 2001), 129–50.

2. *Arch. Md.* 2: 474–88, 493–94, 500–503; *Arch. Md.* 15: 57–62, 65–77.

3. Charles Andrews, ed., *Narratives of the Insurrections, 1675–1690* (New York: Charles Scribner's Sons, 1915), 22; *PWB*, 531.

4. *PWB*, 532; William Sherwood, "Virginia's Deploured Condition," in *Collections of the Massachusetts Historical Society, Fourth Series*, Vol. 9 (1871), 170 (quotation); Warren Billings, *Sir William Berkeley and the Forging of Colonial Virginia* (Baton Rouge: Louisiana State University Press, 2004), 240–43; William Kelso, *Jamestown: The Buried Truth* (Charlottesville: University of Virginia Press, 2006), 208–9.

5. Andrews, *Narratives*, 22–23; *PWB* 532–33, 537, 570, 630.

6. Andrews, *Narratives*, 25–27; Hening, *Statutes* 2: 341–43; Margaret Holmes Williamson, *Powhatan Lords of Life and Death: Command and Consent in Seventeenth-Century Virginia* (Lincoln: University of Nebraska Press, 2003), 247–54.

7. H. R. McIlwaine, *Journals of the House of Burgesses, 1659/60–1693* (Richmond: Colonial Press, 1914), 66.

8. *PWB*, 537; Andrews, *Narratives*, 27–28; Hening, *Statutes*, 2: 341–65; *WMQ* 9 (1900), 8–9.

9. Andrews, *Narratives*, 28–30; Sherwood, "Virginia's Deploured Condition," 171; Michael Oberg, ed., *Samuel Wiseman's Book of Record: The Official Account of Bacon's Rebellion in Virginia, 1676–1677* (Lanham, MD: Lexington Books, 2005), 151–52; *PWB*, 537.

10. Sherwood, "Virginia's Deploured Condition," 172; Hening, *Statutes*, 2: 363–65; Oberg, *Samuel Wiseman's Book of Record*, 152.

11. *PWB*, 535–38.

12. *WMQ* 9 (1900), 5–9; "Bacon's Rebellion," *VMHB* 1 (1893), 170–86.

13. Andrews, *Narratives*, 30–33, 38.

## Chapter 5

1. William Sherwood, "Virginia's Deploured Condition," in *Collections of the Massachusetts Historical Society, Fourth Series*, Vol. 9 (1871), 172–75; Michael Oberg, ed., *Samuel Wiseman's Book of Record: The Official Account of Bacon's Rebellion in Virginia, 1676–1677* (Lanham, MD: Lexington Books, 2005), 154–55, 180; *PWB*, 539–41; Charles Andrews, ed., *Narratives of the Insurrections, 1675–1690* (New York: Charles Scribner's Sons, 1915), 56–57.

2. "Proclamations of Nathaniel Bacon," *VMHB* 1 (1893–94), 55–61; Oberg, *Samuel Wiseman's Book of Record*, 156–58; Andrews, *Narratives*, 60–62.

3. *Arch. Md.* 5: 143, 153; *Arch. Md.* 15: 99, 124–28; David Lovejoy, *The Glorious Revolution in America* (New York: Harper, 1972), 79.

4. Andrews, *Narratives*, 34–35; Sherwood, "Virginia's Deploured Condition," 175; Daphne Gentry, "Arthur Allen," *DVB* 1: 73–75.

5. Sherwood, "Virginia's Deploured Condition," 175–77; Oberg, *Samuel Wiseman's Book of Record*, 158–62, 182; Andrews, *Narratives*, 38.

6. Sherwood, "Virginia's Deploured Condition," 174–75; Oberg, *Samuel Wiseman's Book of Record*, 162, 182, 275; *PWB*, 542–43, 568, 571–72; Andrews, *Narratives*, 65.

7. *PWB*, 572; Andrews, *Narratives*, 65–67.

8. An. Coton, "An Account of Our Late Troubles in Virginia," in Peter Force, ed., *Tracts and Other Papers, Relating Principally to the Origin, Settlement,*

*and Progress of the Colonies in North America, from the Discovery of the Country to the Year 1776* (New York: Peter Smith, 1947), 7–8; Oberg, *Samuel Wiseman's* Book of Record, 162–68, 182–83; Andrews, *Narratives*, 67–70; [?] to [Francis Nicholson], February 20, 1704/05, Francis Nicholson Papers, Mss. 1943.4, John D. Rockefeller, Jr., Library, Colonial Williamsburg Foundation; Wilcomb Washburn, *The Governor and the Rebel: A History of Bacon's Rebellion in Virginia* (Chapel Hill: University of North Carolina Press, 1957), 81, 209.

9. Gentry, "Arthur Allen"; [?] to [Nicholson], February 20, 1704/05, Nicholson Papers.

10. *PWB*, 572; Andrews, *Narratives*, 71; Oberg, *Samuel Wiseman's* Book of Record, 167–68, 183; Andrews, *Narratives*, 35; An. Cotton, "Account of Our Late Troubles," 8; Robert Beverley, *The History and Present State of Virginia*, ed. Louis B. Wright (Chapel Hill: University of North Carolina Press, 1947), 86 (quotations).

## Chapter 6

1. Charles Andrews, ed., *Narratives of the Insurrections, 1675–1690* (New York: Charles Scribner's Sons, 1915), 73–74.

2. Augustine Warner to Philip Ludwell, June 7, 1678, C.O. 1/42, 178–79, VCRP Reel 94; Mary McCurdy, "The Townleys and Warners of Virginia and Their English Connections," *VMHB* 81 (1973), 351–52; Michael Oberg, ed., *Samuel Wiseman's Book of Record: The Official Account of Bacon's Rebellion in Virginia, 1676–1677* (Lanham, MD: Lexington Books, 2005), 278; Lorena Walsh, *Motives of Honor, Pleasure, and Profit: Plantation Management in the Colonial Chesapeake, 1607–1763* (Chapel Hill: University of North Carolina Press, 2010), 178–79.

3. "A Journal of ye Time ye Ship *Young Prince* was in ye Kings Service in James River," C.O. 1/37, 181–86, VCRP reel 92; Oberg, *Samuel Wiseman's* Book of Record, 277–86; Darrett Rutman and Anita Rutman, *A Place in Time: Middlesex County, Virginia, 1650–1750* (New York: Norton, 1984), 81–87; Stephen Saunders Webb, *1676: The End of American Independence* (New York: Knopf, 1984), 89.

4. Oberg, *Samuel Wiseman's* Book of Record, 171, 184; Andrews, *Narratives*, 39, 74–78; *PWB*, 573; "Journal of the *Young Prince*." This diagnosis is conjecture, but typhus is easily the best fit for the symptoms described in contemporary accounts of his death.

5. "Petition and Proposals Respecting Nathaniel Bacon," *VMHB* 1 (1894), 430–31; *PWB*, 544–52 (quotation on 551), 555; Webb, *1676*, 208,

213–19; Wilcomb Washburn, *The Governor and the Rebel: A History of Bacon's Rebellion in Virginia* (Chapel Hill: University of North Carolina Press, 1957), 93–95.

6. "A Journal of . . . *Young Prince*"; Andrews, *Narratives*, 38, 77–78, 92; Oberg, *Samuel Wiseman's* Book of Record, 171; *PWB*, 538; Webb, *1676*, 84–86.

7. Andrews, *Narratives*, 79.

8. "A Journal of . . . *Young Prince*." The identification of John Gatlin is provisional; see "Isle of Wight County Records," *WMQ* 7 (1899), 243–86.

9. *PWB*, 552–54; Andrews, *Narratives*, 79–80.

10. Andrews, *Narratives*, 80–83, 86–91; *PWB*, 573.

11. *Arch. Md.*, 15: 137–41.

12. Andrews, *Narratives*, 92; Thomas Grantham, *An Historical Account of Some Memorable Actions* (London, 1714), 10, 17–19; Grantham to Henry Coventry, Coventry Papers 77: 301–2, VCRP Reel 90; Webb, *1676*, 113–18.

13. Grantham, *Historical Account*, 14–16.

14. Oberg, *Samuel Wiseman's* Book of Record, 184, 275–76; Journal of the *Young Prince*; [?] to [Francis Nicholson], February 20, 1704/05, Francis Nicholson Papers, Mss. 1943.4, John D. Rockefeller, Jr., Library, Colonial Williamsburg Foundation; "Bacon's Men in Surry," *VMHB* 5 (1898), 373.

15. Grantham to Coventry; Andrews, *Narratives*, 93–98 (quotations on 93, 96); *PWB*, 560–61; Journal of the *Young Prince*; Rutman and Rutman, *Place in Time*, 81.

16. Deposition of William Overton, C.O. 1/42, 179, VCRP Reel 94.

17. "A Journal of . . . *Young Prince*"; Andrews, *Narratives*, 98; *PWB*, 563; Oberg, *Samuel Wiseman's* Book of Record, 184–85.

18. Andrews, *Narratives*, 39; An. Coton, "An Account of Our Late Troubles in Virginia," in Peter Force, ed., *Tracts and Other Papers, Relating Principally to the Origin, Settlement, and Progress of the Colonies in North America, from the Discovery of the Country to the Year 1776* (New York: Peter Smith, 1947), 9–10.

## Chapter 7

1. "Bristol Log," January 28–31, 1676/7, ADM 51/134, VCRP Reel 647; *PWB*, 551–52, 565; Michael Oberg, ed., *Samuel Wiseman's Book of Record: The Official Account of Bacon's Rebellion in Virginia, 1676–1677* (Lanham, MD: Lexington Books, 2005), 54, 30–62.

2. *PWB*, 566–67.

3. *PWB*, 568–73, 579; "Bristol Log."

4. H. R. McIlwaine, *Journals of the House of Burgesses of Virginia, 1659/60–1693* (Richmond: Colonial Press, 1914), 68–94; Hening, *Statutes* 2: 366–406.

5. Oberg, *Samuel Wiseman's Book of Record*, 98–99, 130, 134–41; C. S. Everett, "'They shalbe slaves for their lives': Indian Slavery in Colonial Virginia," in Alan Gallay, ed., *Indian Slavery in Colonial America* (Lincoln: University of Nebraska Press, 2009), 67–107; Stephen Saunders Webb, *1676: The End of American Independence* (New York: Knopf, 1984), 147–48.

6. *PWB*, 613; Warren Billings, *Sir William Berkeley and the Forging of Colonial Virginia* (Baton Rouge: Louisiana State University Press, 2004), chs. 14–15.

7. Oberg, *Samuel Wiseman's* Book of Record, 104, 173–77, 190–91; *PWB*, 584–85; 596–98.

8. Oberg, *Samuel Wiseman's* Book of Record, 66–67, 86, 98–107, 128, 173–75, 191 (quotations on 98, 103); *PWB*, 577, 597, 601–2 (quotation).

9. Oberg, *Samuel Wiseman's* Book of Record, 108–9; *PWB*, 607–10, 633.

10. *PWB*, 578–79, 583, 598–99.

11. *PWB*, 608–10, 614, 633; Billings, *Sir William Berkeley*, 268; Wilcomb Washburn, *The Governor and the Rebel: A History of Bacon's Rebellion in Virginia* (Chapel Hill: University of North Carolina Press, 1957), 139.

12. Coventry Papers, 77: 449–50, VCRP Reel 901; *PWB*, 611–13.

13. Oberg, *Samuel Wiseman's* Book of Record, 118–19 (quotation), 142–85, 275–77; Brent Tarter, "Bacon's Rebellion, the Grievances of the People, and the Political Culture of Seventeenth-Century Virginia," *VMHB* 119 (2011), 2–41.

## Chapter 8

1. C.O. 1/36, 213–18, VCRP Reel 92. An error-ridden transcription is published in *Arch. Md.* 5: 134–52.

2. *Arch. Md.* 5: 152–54, 244–49, 269; Stephen Saunders Webb, *1676: The End of American Independence* (New York: Knopf, 1984), 385.

3. Baltimore to William Blathwayt, July 14, 1679, CO 1/43, 161–62, VCRP Reel 94 (quotation); *DRCHSNY* 3: 277 (quotation); Matthew Lawson Rhoades, "Assarigoa's Line: Anglo-Iroquois Origins of the Virginia Frontier, 1675–1774" (Ph.D. diss., Syracuse, 2000), 32–35.

4. *Arch. Md.* 15: 236–42.

5. Rhoades, "Assarigoa's Line," 34–36; Lawrence Leder, ed., *The Livingston Indian Records, 1666–1723* (Gettysburg: Pennsylvania Historical Association, 1956), 48–61.

6. *Arch. Md.* 15: 277–314, 329–31.

7. Hening, *Statutes* 2: 346, 404, 440, 490–92; Robbie Ethridge, *From Chicaza to Chicasaw: The European Invasion and the Transformation of the Mississippian World, 1540–1715* (Chapel Hill: University of North Carolina Press, 2010), 99–115; C. S. Everett, "'They shalbe slaves for their lives': Indian Slavery in Colonial Virginia," in Alan Gallay, ed., *Indian Slavery in Colonial America* (Lincoln: University of Nebraska Press, 2009), 67–107; April Hatfield, *Atlantic Virginia: Intercolonial Relations in the Seventeenth Century* (Philadelphia: University of Pennsylvania Press, 2004), 24–32; Paul Kelton, *Epidemics and Enslavement: Biological Catastrophe in the Native Southeast, 1492–1715* (Lincoln: University of Nebraska Press, 2007), 108–15.

8. Eric Bowne, *The Westo Indians: Slave Traders of the Early Colonial South* (Tuscaloosa: University of Alabama Press, 2005), chs. 7–8; Alan Gallay, *The Indian Slave Trade: The Rise of the English Empire in the American South, 1670–1717* (New Haven: Yale University Press, 2002), ch. 3.

9. Tim Harris, *Restoration: Charles II and His Kingdoms* (New York: Penguin Books, 2005), 68–84.

10. J. P. Kenyon, *The Popish Plot* (London: Heinemann, 1972), chs. 1–3 (quotation on 96); Tim Harris, *Revolutions: The Great Crisis of the British Monarchy, 1685–1720* (London: Allen Lane, 2005), 31.

11. *Arch. Md.* 5: 281, 319; *Arch. Md.* 15: 244–50; David Lovejoy, *The Glorious Revolution in America* (New York: Harper & Row, 1972), 84.

## Chapter 9

1. *Arch. Md.* 15: 364–73, 411–20.

2. *Arch. Md.* 5: 320–23.

3. *Arch. Md.* 15: 353, 359, 373–74, 380, 382–86, 400, 408 (quotations on 353, 380, 408).

4. *Arch. Md.* 5: 280–82; *Arch. Md.* 15: 391–92, 399–411.

5. *Arch. Md.* 5: 311–34.

6. Warren Billings, *The Old Dominion in the Seventeenth Century: A Documentary History of Virginia, 1606–1700*, rev. ed. (Chapel Hill: University of North Carolina Press, 2007), 349–55; *Executive Journals*, 18–41

(quotation on 41), 48; *Arch. Md.* 5: 357; Spencer to Sir Lyonel Jenkins, August 12, 1682, C.O. 1/49, 106–7, VCRP Reel 96.

7. Richard Beale Davis, ed., *William Fitzhugh and His Chesapeake World, 1676–1701* (Chapel Hill: University of North Carolina Press, 1963), 93; Marion Tinling, ed., *The Correspondence of the Three William Byrds of Westover, Virginia, 1684–1776* (Charlottesville: University Press of Virginia, 1977) 1: 14–15, 29, 31; John Coombs, "Beyond the Origins Debate: Rethinking the Rise of Virginia Slavery," in Douglas Bradburn and John C. Coombs, eds., *Early Modern Virginia: Reconsidering the Old Dominion* (Charlottesville: University of Virginia Press, 2011), 239–78; Edmund S. Morgan, *American Slavery, American Freedom: The Ordeal of Colonial Virginia* (New York: Norton, 1975), 330.

8. Hening, *Statutes*, 2: 490–93; H. R. McIlwaine, ed., *Journals of the House of Burgesses of Virginia, 1659/60–1693* (Richmond, 1914), 174.

9. Effingham sent William Byrd to Albany to renew the treaty less than a year later. *The Papers of Francis Howard, Baron Howard of Effingham, 1643–1695*, ed. Warren Billings (Richmond: Library of Virginia, 1989), 46–51, 110–23, 142–51, 212–13 (quotations on 123, 151); *Byrds*, 1: 55.

10. John McNeill, *Mosquito Empires: Ecology and War in the Greater Caribbean, 1620–1914* (New York: Cambridge University Press, 2010), 72–73.

11. Tim Harris, *Restoration: Charles II and His Kingdoms* (New York: Allen Lane, 2005) (quotations on 287–89); Harris, *Revolution: The Great Crisis of the British Monarchy, 1685–1720* (New York: Allen Lane, 2006), 1–93 (quotation on 407).

12. *Effingham*, 224–28, 235, 240; Herbert Paschal, ed., "George Bancroft's 'Lost Notes' on the General Court Records of Seventeenth-Century Virginia," *VMHB* 91 (1983), 356.

13. David Lovejoy, *The Glorious Revolution in America* (New York: Harper & Row, 1972), 87, 258.

14. Martha McCartney, "Cockacoeske, Queen of the Pamunkey," in Gregory Waselkov et al., eds., *Powhatan's Mantle: Indians in the Colonial Southeast*, rev. ed. (Lincoln: University of Nebraska Press, 2006), 259–60.

## Chapter 10

1. Marion Tinling, ed., *The Correspondence of the Three William Byrds of Westover, Virginia, 1684–1776* (Charlottesville: University Press of Virginia, 1977), 1: 89–90.

2. *The Papers of Francis Howard, Baron Howard of Effingham, 1643–1695*, ed. Warren Billings (Richmond: Library of Virginia, 1989), 399; David Lovejoy, *The Glorious Revolution in America* (New York: Harper & Row, 1972), 238, 260.

3. Steven Pincus, *England's Glorious Revolution, 1688–1689: A Brief History with Documents* (Boston: Bedford/St. Martin's Press, 2006), 35–43.

4. Tim Harris, *Revolution: The Great Crisis of the British Monarchy, 1685–1720* (New York: Allen Lane, 2006), ch. 7; Martin Quitt, "Sir John Berry," *DVB* 1: 461–62; Lovejoy, *The Glorious Revolution*, 264–65.

5. *Arch. Md.* 13: 147–53; *Executive Journals*, 100–101, 103–7.

6. *Arch. Md.* 8: 70–94.

7. *Arch. Md.* 8: 101–9, 116, 123–24; Charles Andrews, *Narratives of the Insurrections, 1675–1690* (New York: Charles Scribner's Sons, 1915), 40; Beverly McAnear, "Mariland's Grevances Wiy The Have Taken Up Arms," *Journal of Southern History* 8 (1942), 404.

8. McAnear, "Mariland's Grevances," 406; *Arch. Md.* 8: 106–57.

## Chapter 11

1. *Arch. Md.* 8: 162, 167; *Arch. Md.* 13: 240; David Lovejoy, *The Glorious Revolution in America* (New York: Harper, 1972), chs. 15–19.

2. Marion Tinling, ed., *The Correspondence of the Three William Byrds of Westover, Virginia, 1684–1776* (Charlottesville: University Press of Virginia, 1977) 1: 114–65 (quotations on 121–22, 137).

3. Unless otherwise noted, this section follows Stephen Saunders Webb's "The Strange Career of Francis Nicholson," *WMQ* 23 (1966), 513–48. See also Bruce McCully, "From the North Riding to Morocco: The Early Years of Francis Nicholson, 1655–1688," *WMQ* 19 (1962), 534–56, and McCully, "Governor Francis Nicholson, Patron *Par Excellence* of Religion and Learning in Colonial America," *WMQ* 39 (1982): 310–33.

4. James D. Kornwolf, "'Doing Good to Posterity': Francis Nicholson, First Patron of Architecture, Landscape Design, and Town Planning in Virginia, Maryland, and South Carolina, 1688–1725," *VMHB* 101 (1993), 333–74.

5. Kornwolf, "'Doing Good to Posterity,'" 364–69.

6. The excavation of Bacon's home is thoroughly documented in the Curles Papers, Virginia Department of Historic Resources, Richmond. See also L. Daniel Mouer, "In the Realm of 'The Rebel': The Archaeology of

Nathaniel Bacon's Brick House at Curles Plantation," *Henrico County Historical Society Magazine* 12 (1988), 3–20.

7. *Executive Journals*, 419.

8. Helen Rountree, *Pocahontas's People: The Powhatan Indians of Virginia through Four Centuries* (Norman: University of Oklahoma Press, 1990), 105–27.

9. Paul Kelton, *Epidemics and Enslavement: Biological Catastrophe in the Native Southeast, 1492–1715* (Lincoln: University of Nebraska Press, 2007); Andros to Lords of Trade, July 1, 1697, C.O. 5/1309, VCRP Reel 35.

10. James Rice, *Nature and History in the Potomac Country: From Hunter-Gatherers to the Age of Jefferson* (Baltimore, MD: Johns Hopkins University Press, 2009), ch. 9.

11. H. R. McIlwaine, *Journals of the House of Burgesses of Virginia, 1702/3–1705, 1705–1706, 1710–1712* (Richmond: Virginia State Library, 1912), 97–98; Rountree, *Pocahontas's People*, 120–21.

12. *Executive Journals*, 147; Kelton, *Epidemics and Enslavement*, 109–43; Rountree, *Pocahontas's People*, 138–40.

13. Kelton, *Epidemics and Enslavement*, 124–25, 143–59; Robbie Ethridge, *From Chicaza to Chickasaw: The European Invasion and the Transformation of the Mississippian World, 1540–1715* (Chapel Hill: University of North Carolina Press, 2010), ch. 6; Allan Gallay, *The Indian Slave Trade: The Rise of the English Empire in the American South, 1670–1717* (New Haven, CT: Yale University Press, 2002), 294–99; John Coombs, "Beyond the Origins Debate: Rethinking the Rise of Virginia Slavery," in Douglas Bradburn and John C. Coombs, eds., *Early Modern Virginia: Reconsidering the Old Dominion* (Charlottesville: University of Virginia Press, 2011), 240–78.

14. Coombs, "Beyond the Origins Debate"; Ira Berlin, *Many Thousands Gone: The First Two Centuries of Slavery in North America* (Cambridge, MA: Harvard University Press, 1998), 110; Lorena Walsh, *Motives of Honor, Pleasure, and Profit: Plantation Management in the Colonial Chesapeake, 1607–1763* (Chapel Hill: University of North Carolina Press, 2010), 131–44, 194–210; Allan Kulikoff, *Tobacco and Slaves: The Development of Southern Cultures in the Chesapeake, 1680–1800* (Chapel Hill: University of North Carolina Press, 1986), ch. 6.

15. Hening, *Statutes*, 3: 252, 298, 447–62; Erwin Surrency, "Revision of Colonial Laws," *American Journal of Legal History* 9 (1965), 189–202; Rountree, *Pocahontas's People*, 142–43.

16. Charles Andrews, *Narratives of the Insurrections, 1675–1690* (New York: Charles Scribner's Sons, 1915), 9–40; "Notes and Queries," *VMHB* 1 (1893), 201–2; "Virginia Gleanings in England," *VMHB* 15 (1907), 57.

17. Robert Beverley, *The History and Present State of Virginia, 1705*, ed. Louis B. Wright (Chapel Hill: University of North Carolina Press, 1947), 74–78, 159–233 (quotations on 75, 78, 232–33); Rountree, *Pocahontas's People*, 109.

18. David Bushnell, "The Account of Lamhatty," *American Anthropologist* 10 (1908), 568–74; Stephen Warren and Randolph Noe, "'The Greatest Travelers in America': Shawnee Survival in the Shatter Zone," in Robbie Ethridge and Sheri Shuck-Hall, eds., *Mapping the Mississippian Shatter Zone: The Colonial Indian Slave Trade and Regional Instability in the American South* (Lincoln: University of Nebraska Press, 2009), 169–76.

## Afterword

1. Wilcomb Washburn, *The Governor and the Rebel: A History of Bacon's Rebellion in Virginia* (Chapel Hill: University of North Carolina Press, 1957), ch. 1.

2. Thomas Wertenbaker, *Torchbearer of the Revolution: The Story of Bacon's Rebellion and Its Leader* (Princeton, NJ: Princeton University Press, 1940), 14, 34, 211.

3. Washburn, *The Governor*, vii, ch. 1; Brent Tarter, "Bacon's Rebellion, the Grievances of the People, and the Political Culture of Seventeenth-Century Virginia," *VMHB* 119 (2011), 6.

4. Washburn, *The Governor*, 163.

5. Webb, *1676: The End of American Independence* (New York: Knopf, 1984). Tarter, "Bacon's Rebellion," 6–9, efficiently summarizes recent debates. See also Kathleen Brown, *Good Wives, Nasty Wenches, and Anxious Patriarchs: Gender, Race, and Power in Colonial Virginia* (Chapel Hill: University of North Carolina Press, 1996), and Anthony Parent, *Foul Means: The Formation of a Slave Society in Virginia, 1660–1740* (Chapel Hill: University of North Carolina Press, 2003).

6. David Lodge, *The Art of Fiction* (New York: Penguin Books, 1992), 155.

7. Carl von Clausewitz, *On War*, trans. J. J. Graham (New York: Barnes & Noble, 1968), 2: 105–6.

8. Jane Smiley, *Thirteen Ways of Looking at the Novel* (New York: Anchor Books, 2005), 251.

9. Robbie Ethridge, *From Chicaza to Chicasaw: The European Invasion and the Transformation of the Mississippian World, 1540–1715* (Chapel Hill: University of North Carolina Press, 2010), 232.

10. Samuel Hazard, ed., *Colonial Records of Pennsylvania* (Harrisburg and Philadelphia: T. Fenn, 1838–1853), 3: 89.

11. Linda Colley, *Britons: Forging the Nation, 1707–1837* (New Haven, CT: Yale University Press, 1992), 1–54 (quotations on 5–6); Owen Stanwood, *The Empire Reformed: English America in the Age of the Glorious Revolution* (Philadelphia: University of Pennsylvania Press, 2011); Douglas Bradburn, "The Visible Fist: The Chesapeake Tobacco Trade in War and the Purpose of Empire, 1690–1715," *WMQ* 68 (2011), 332–60.

12. Edmund S. Morgan, *American Slavery, American Freedom: The Ordeal of Colonial Virginia* (New York: Norton, 1975), 269–70, 344; Alan Taylor, *American Colonies* (New York: Viking/Penguin, 2001), 243.

13. Brown, *Good Wives* (quotation on 186).

# Select Bibliography

## Bacon's Rebellion

Andrews, Charles. *Narratives of the Insurrections, 1675–1690*. New York: Charles Scribner's Sons, 1915.

Oberg, Michael, ed. *Samuel Wiseman's Book of Record: The Official Account of Bacon's Rebellion in Virginia, 1676–1677*. Lanham, MD: Lexington Books, 2005.

Tarter, Brent. "Bacon's Rebellion, the Grievances of the People, and the Political Culture of Seventeenth-Century Virginia." *Virginia Magazine of History and Biography* 119 (2011), 4–41.

Washburn, Wilcomb E. *The Governor and the Rebel: A History of Bacon's Rebellion in Virginia*. Chapel Hill: University of North Carolina Press, 1957.

Webb, Stephen Saunders. *1676: The End of American Independence*. New York: Knopf, 1984.

Wertenbaker, Thomas Jefferson. *Torchbearer of the Revolution: The Story of Bacon's Rebellion and Its Leader*. Princeton, NJ: Princeton University Press, 1940.

## Colonial Chesapeake Society

Billings, Warren. *A Little Parliament: The Virginia General Assembly in the Seventeenth Century*. Richmond: Library of Virginia, 2004.

———. *Sir William Berkeley and the Forging of Colonial Virginia*. Baton Rouge: Louisiana State University Press, 2004.

Bradburn, Douglas, and John C. Coombs, eds. *Early Modern Virginia: Reconsidering the Old Dominion*. Charlottesville: University of Virginia Press, 2011.

Brown, Kathleen. *Good Wives, Nasty Wenches, and Anxious Patriarchs: Gender, Race, and Power in Colonial Virginia*. Chapel Hill: University of North Carolina Press, 1996.

Carr, Lois Green, Philip D. Morgan, and Jean B. Russo, eds. *Colonial Chesapeake Society*. Chapel Hill: University of North Carolina Press, 1988.

Morgan, Edmund S. *American Slavery, American Freedom: The Ordeal of Colonial Virginia*. New York: Norton, 1975.

Walsh, Lorena. *Motives of Honor, Pleasure, and Profit: Plantation Management in the Colonial Chesapeake, 1607–1763*. Chapel Hill: University of North Carolina Press, 2010.

## Native America

Ethridge, Robbie. *From Chicaza to Chickasaw: The European Invasion and the Transformation of the Mississippian World, 1540–1715*. Chapel Hill: University of North Carolina Press, 2010.

Gallay, Alan, ed. *Indian Slavery in Colonial America*. Lincoln: University of Nebraska Press, 2009.

Oberg, Michael. *Dominion and Civility: English Imperialism and Native America, 1585–1685*. Ithaca, NY: Cornell University Press, 2004.

Rice, James. *Nature and History in the Potomac Country: From Hunter-Gatherers to the Age of Jefferson*. Baltimore, MD: Johns Hopkins University Press, 2009.

Richter, Daniel K. *Facing East from Indian Country: A Native History of Early America*. Cambridge, MA: Harvard University Press, 2001.

Rountree, Helen. *Pocahontas's People: The Powhatan Indians of Virginia through Four Centuries*. Norman: University of Oklahoma Press, 1990.

## Britain and Its American Colonies

Brewer, John. *The Sinews of Power: War, Money, and the English State, 1688–1783*. New York: Knopf, 1989.

Craven, Wesley Frank. *The Southern Colonies in the Seventeenth Century*. Baton Rouge: Louisiana State University Press, 1949.

Harris, Tim. *Restoration: Charles II and His Kingdoms, 1660–1685.* New York: Allen Lane, 2006.

——. *Revolution: The Great Crisis of the British Monarchy, 1685–1720.* New York: Allen Lane, 2006.

Pincus, Steven. *1688: The First Modern Revolution.* New Haven, CT: Yale University Press, 2009.

Stanwood, Owen. *The Empire Reformed: English America in the Age of the Glorious Revolution.* Philadelphia: University of Pennsylvania Press, 2011.

Taylor, Alan. *American Colonies.* New York: Viking/Penguin, 2001.

# INDEX